Orange County Place Names
A to Z

Orange County Place Names
A to Z

Phil Brigandi

"Adventures in the Natural History and Cultural Heritage of the Californias"

Sunbelt Publications, Inc.

San Diego, California

Orange County Place Names A to Z
Sunbelt Publications, Inc.
Copyright © 2006 by the author
All rights reserved. First edition 2006

Edited by Jennifer Redmond
Cover design by Armadillo Creative
Composition by W.G. Hample and Associates
Project management by Jennifer Redmond
Printed in the United States of America

No part of this book may be reproduced in any form without permission from the publisher. Please direct comments and inquiries to:

Sunbelt Publications, Inc.
P.O. Box 191126
San Diego, CA 92159-1126
(619) 258-4911, fax: (619) 258-4916
www.sunbeltbooks.com

10 09 08 07 06   5 4 3 2 1

Library of Congress Cataloging-in-Publication Data

Brigandi, Phil, 1959-
  Orange County place names, A to Z / Phil Brigandi. — 1st ed.
     p. cm.
  Includes bibliographical references.
  ISBN-13: 978-0-932653-79-6
  ISBN-10: 0-932653-79-0
  1. Names, Geographical—California—Orange County. 2. Orange
County (Calif.)—History, Local. I. Title.

F868.O6B75 2006
917.94'96—dc22

                                                    2006009687

Contents

Introduction   *vii*

A (Very) Brief History of Orange County   *ix*

Orange County Place Names A-Z   *1*

Acknowledgments   *109*

Selected Bibliography   *111*

our pass. This book is an attempt to ... and serve them with ...

Columns ... lived the ...
But while some names spread, others diminish ...
"Santa Ana" was used to describe the coastal plain from Newport
Bay up over the hills into the Pomona Valley ...
the years before the county was formed ...

Introduction

Every place name is a story. In them, we see reminders of the eras, activities, and personalities that make up our local history. Understanding their origin and meaning helps us to better understand our past. This book is an attempt to capture a few of those stories, and share them with county residents both old and new.

But what exactly is a place name? Some scholars insist on purely geographical names — names of cities, towns, rivers, mountains, and streams. But in a modern, suburban area such as Orange County, place names take on many other forms. We speak of places "over by Disneyland," or "below the El Toro Y." Some names may have never appeared on a map, but are used as place names none the less. Our towns and cities are broken down into scores of communities and neighborhoods. The City of Santa Ana counts more than 50 separate neighborhoods within its boundaries, and Newport Beach is a patchwork of communities stretching from West Newport to the Newport Coast, with stops along the way in Corona del Mar, Balboa, East Bluff, and half a dozen islands. Their names are part of what give these neighborhoods their identity.

Place names come in many forms. They can be descriptive (Emerald Bay, Carbon Canyon, Bolsa Chica), they can commemorate a person or event (Trabuco Canyon, Silverado, Huntington Beach), they can be transplanted from other areas (Delhi, Las Flores), or they can simply be the product of human imagination (Coast Royal, Corona del Mar). Other place names are borrowed from earlier names. Thus the various "lagunas" that have spread out across the South County, far from the original lakes named during the mission days.

But while some names spread, others diminish. In mission times, "Santa Ana" was used to describe the coastal plain from Newport Bay up over the hills into the Pomona Valley and out to Chino. In the years before the county was formed, what would become Orange County was generally known as the Santa Ana Valley. Today that name is almost extinct. Many other early place names only survive as the names of streets, parks, or schools.

I have chosen to take a broad approach in selecting the names for this book. I have tried to include all the major place names currently in use in the county, along with those historic names that may have faded from view but are still significant. Other names are included for what they can teach us about our local history, or simply for the pleasure of spinning a good yarn.

Many other historians have explored our local place names over the years. In the early 1930s, Terry Stephenson wrote two interesting articles about Orange County place names. Erwin Gudde's *California Place Names* (first published in 1949 and now in its fourth edition) has been a standard work for more than half a century. Other local historians have discussed place names while writing about their own communities.

But it was the late Don Meadows who compiled the only full-length study of the subject, *Historic Place Names of Orange County* (1966). I freely acknowledge my debt to my old friend and mentor — and also to Don's family, who have allowed me to quote freely from his work.

It has been said that there are two kinds of books — perfect books, and books that actually get published. I have opted for the latter. More research will continue to uncover additional information about our local place names, but in the meantime, I hope this book will prove useful as an interim report.

To keep things simple, I have identified any quotes by the name of the author, the publication date, and a page number (Meadows, 1966:1). You can find a complete citation in the Selected Bibliography at the end of this book.

I have tried to group together similar names, and keep cross-references to a minimum. Many entries also mention other place names, and more information can be found in those listings. To save space, I only give locations for places not readily available from modern sources, such as the Thomas Guide street atlas, or topographical maps. In the same way, any Spanish-English dictionary will translate most of the common Spanish words that remain a part of our local place names.

If this book can help to spread a greater awareness and appreciation of Orange County's rich history, I will be grateful. If it encourages even one other person to begin their own research into our past, my efforts will have been richly rewarded.

— *Phil Brigandi*

A (Very) Brief History of Orange County

Indians lived here for centuries before the first Spanish explorers entered Orange County in 1769. Within a few years, the missions San Gabriel (1771) and San Juan Capistrano (1776) had laid claim to much of the area. A few grazing concessions were given to retired soldiers before the end of Spanish rule in 1821, but it was not until the Mexican government secularized the missions in the 1830s that the Rancho Era truly began. By the start of the Mexican War in 1846, nearly all of Orange County except the mountain regions had been granted to the rancheros.

These great cattle ranches were the backbone of the local economy until the drought of 1863-64. The only communities worthy of the name were at San Juan Capistrano and Old Santa Ana (Olive). Then in 1857, a group of Germans immigrants living in San Francisco joined together in a cooperative venture to found an agricultural community they named Anaheim.

Two events in 1868 opened up much of the Santa Ana Valley to settlers. South and east of the Santa Ana River, the old Rancho Santiago de Santa Ana — long the stronghold of the Yorba and Peralta families — was broken up and divided among scores of individual owners. While on the other side of the river, debt forced Abel Stearns to place most of his extensive landholdings into the hands of a trust. The Los Angeles & San Bernardino Land Company began offering thousands of acres of the Stearns Ranchos for sale. New towns sprang up almost immediately on both sides of the river — Santa Ana, Tustin, Orange, Westminster, Garden Grove — and settlers spread out across the land.

The Southern Pacific railroad arrived in the mid-1870s, but it was not until the Santa Fe completed a direct transcontinental link into Southern California that the full impact of the railroads was felt. Competition between the two railroads helped to launch Southern California's greatest real estate boom. During the frantic "Boom of the Eighties" (1886-88), scores of subdivisions were platted and more than a dozen new towns were laid out here. But the Boom collapsed as quickly as it had begun, and only Fullerton, Buena Park, and El Toro survived to become incorporated cities.

The Boom also led to the creation of Orange County in 1889. It had been almost 20 years since the first proposal to split off the southern end of Los Angeles County had been sent to Sacramento. The flush years of the Boom and the rise in population gave the Santa Ana Valley the financial and political clout it needed to finally form its own county.

As Orange County moved into the 20th century, transportation continued to play a key role in our development. Between 1905 and 1910, the Pacific Electric Railway built three main lines into Orange County — one along the coast from Seal Beach to Balboa, a second across the center of the valley through Cypress and Garden Grove on its way to Santa Ana, and a third to serve the northern communities of La Habra, Brea, and Yorba Linda. The PE's "big red cars" brought a surge of new townsites and subdivisions along the tracks.

Beginning around 1915, the automobile also started to have an impact. As good roads were built through the county, development followed. By the mid-1920s the bigger cities — Santa Ana, Anaheim, Fullerton, Huntington Beach — were surrounded by smaller tracts and townsites out on the highways.

Railroads, red cars, roads, and eventually freeways; wherever they led, development always followed.

The county's economy remained largely agricultural until the 1950s. Not just oranges, but lemons, apricots, walnuts, lima beans, celery, sugar beets, and avocados all thrived here. Other farmers grew wheat, barley, tomatoes, strawberries, or other row crops, kept dairy cattle, or raised chickens.

Oil also helped to fuel Orange County's growth. From a small beginning in the 1880s along the northern edge of the county, the oil industry burst into prominence in 1919-20, when major strikes were made at Placentia and Huntington Beach. Soon thousands of wells dotted the county, from the northern foothills right down to the water's edge along the coast.

Yet by 1940, Orange County's population was still only 130,000, while California was nearing 7,000,000.

World War II would help to change all that. Huge military installations were established throughout the county, and thousands of men and women passed through here on their way overseas.

After the war, many returned to settle here. The post-war boom hit Orange County with a vengeance in the 1950s, and communities like Garden Grove and Buena Park grew at an incredible rate. By 1963, Orange County's population had passed the one million mark.

But to the south, things went on pretty much as they always had. Most of the southern third of the county was held by a few large ranch owners — the Irvines, the O'Neills, the Moultons, and others. Cattle ranching and farming were still king in the South County as late as 1960. But as imported water became available, and the Santa Ana Freeway pushed south towards San Diego, the big ranches started being developed as master planned communities, and the South County began to shine.

Today, high tech, light industry, and the service sector have replaced agriculture as the basis of our economy. Much of Orange County has been built up, but many new tracts and new developments are still yet to come — and with them will come even more Orange County place names.

Orange County Place Names A-Z

A

Abbotts Landing. Edward J. Abbott (1843-1895) is said to have built the first house in what is now Balboa in the late 1880s. He dug a freshwater well into the sand (as unlikely as that sounds), and around 1890 built a little pier out into the bay near Palm Street, about where the Balboa Island Ferry now sets sail. The spot became known as Abbotts Landing. In the early 1890s, he ran tourists around the bay in his little steam launch, the *Last Chance*.

Adobe Station. An old adobe building on the Rancho San Joaquín, later used as a stop on the early stage lines between Los Angeles and San Diego. At least one old timer remembered it as the Red Hill Station. The adobe fell into ruin around 1880. It was located southeast of Bryan and Browning avenues in Tustin.

Aegean Hills. A residential area in the Saddleback Valley, developed over a number of years beginning in the 1960s. The Aegean Sea lies between Greece and Turkey, and the name appears in various forms on both sides of the water — though no one seems to be able to agree on the name's origin.

Agua Chinon Canyon (or Wash). A small canyon that drains south from the top of Limestone Canyon. According to Terry Stephenson, the name actually belongs on the other side of the divide. In the 1850s, Limestone Canyon "was known as Cañada de Aguaje del Chinon, Canyon of Curly's Spring. A Negro nicknamed Curly lived at the springs" (1932:111). Agua Chinon Canyon is shown as Tomato Springs Canyon on some old maps. *See* **Chino Hills**.

Airplane Hill. Actually a dip on Ellis Avenue between Goldenwest and Gothard streets in Huntington Beach. It was well known to county drivers in the 1930s. When hit at the right speed, it could launch a car into the air — sometimes with disastrous results. The trick worked best driving east, but don't bother trying it — the dip has long since been filled.

Alamitos. An early school district, established in 1878. The name means "little cottonwoods" in Spanish, and may be borrowed from the nearby Rancho Los Alamitos. The Alamitos School was located on the site of Hare Elementary School in Garden Grove. The Alamitos Friends Church, founded 1891, was another central point in the community. The school district became part of the Garden Grove Unified School District in 1965, and the church is now the Garden Grove Friends Church.

Alamitos Bay. Prior to 1825, the Santa Ana River drained into the ocean here, on the edge of the Rancho Los Alamitos. *See* **Anaheim Landing**.

Aliso. A station on the Santa Fe Railroad where it crossed Newport Avenue, south of Tustin. It was active from 1888 to 1903. "In Spanish dictionaries, the word 'aliso' is given as 'alder.' The reports left by the Portolá explorers use the word frequently for 'sycamore,' and from that earliest expedition of Spaniards into California, the word has meant sycamore in California" (Stephenson, 1932:110). The area around Tustin was noted for its native sycamore trees, which probably gave this point its name. *See* **Sycamore**.

Aliso. A school district formed in 1886 to serve the foothill area north of Lake Forest. The district was suspended in 1905 and annexed to the Trabuco district. The name comes from the Rancho Cañada de los Alisos. **Aliso Beach**. A seaside camping area at the mouth of Aliso Creek, popular as far back as the 1890s. The County of Orange began acquiring property here in 1949, and it is now a part of the county park system. The county once had a pier here, but it has since been removed. **Aliso City**. A failed townsite laid out during the Boom days of 1887. When the Boom collapsed, the townsite faded. It was located along the Santa Fe tracks at El Toro Road. The post office here used the older name of El Toro, and that name soon replaced Aliso City. Today the area is part of the City of Lake Forest. **Aliso Creek**. Like most of the Aliso names in this area, the creek was named for the Rancho Cañada de los Alisos. It forms the southeastern boundary of the rancho. **Aliso Viejo**. The Mission Viejo Company bought the last 6,600 acres of the old Moulton Ranch in 1976 and began work on a new master planned community here. The name combines Aliso Creek, which runs through the area, with the Mission Viejo Company's name. The first residents arrived in 1982. In 2001 the area incorporated as the City of Aliso Viejo.

Almond. The first stop on the Southern Pacific Railroad as it entered Orange County. It was located where the tracks crossed Orangethorpe Avenue near Dale Avenue, in Buena Park. It was originally known as Metcalfs, then (in the early 1880s) as Costa, and finally (by 1890) as Almond. It mostly served as a shipping point for local farmers, but in the early 1900s it also had a small bench shelter for passengers. The station was officially abandoned in 1940.

Alta Vista. A Mexican citrus worker camp located on high ground north of Imperial Highway and west of Walnut Street in La Habra. The name was in use by the 1930s. There was also once a little cluster of vacation cabins on the Orange/Riverside county line near the top of the Santa Ana Canyon known as Alta Vista, and a 1920s tract below Newport Beach was known as Alta Vista Shores.

Amerige Heights. A residential and commercial development on the former site of Hughes Aircraft, northeast of Gilbert Street and Malvern Avenue in the City of Fullerton. Hughes opened here in 1958 on what was then known as Coyote Mesa. The new development was named after the founders of Fullerton, brothers George and Edward Amerige. The 290-acre tract opened in 2001.

Anaheim. Orange County's first city was founded in 1857 as a cooperative agricultural venture by German immigrants living in San Francisco. The first settlers arrived in 1859, a post office was established in 1861, and the school district was formed in 1867. The name was selected by a vote of the colonists, and signifies their new home (*heim* in German) along the Santa Ana River. Theodore Schmidt is usually credited with suggesting the name, which narrowly beat out Annagau, the district (*gau*) on the Santa Ana. Their Spanish-speaking neighbors called the new town Campo Aleman (German Camp). The original townsite was bounded by what are still known as North, South, East, and West streets. On a map, the townsite appears tilted because it was laid out to follow the irrigation ditch instead of the government survey lines. The city was first incorporated from 1870 to 1872, and reincorporated in 1876. By the 1880s, the city had been nicknamed the "Mother Colony." **Anaheim Hills**. In 1970, 4,200 acres of the Nohl Ranch were bought up by a group of developers for $10,000,000. A planned community was built here, stretching across the Bixby Hills on the south side of the Santa Ana Canyon. The City of Anaheim had been annexing territory on that side of the river since the early 1960s, giving the new development its name. **Anaheim Landing**. The original Anaheim Landing was established on Alamitos Bay in 1864 as a shipping point for the colony. There was no wharf, so ships would anchor offshore, and the cargo was floated in on smaller boats, called lighters. After the floods of 1867 shifted the mouth of the San Gabriel River, Anaheim Landing was moved a mile-and-a-half down the coast to what is still known as Anaheim Bay. The landing remained an important shipping point until the Southern Pacific reached Anaheim in 1875, then began a long decline. It was a beachfront resort in the early 20th century. In the 1920s, the Pacific Electric had a stop at Anaheim Landing. The area is now a part of the Seal Beach Naval Weapons Station, and is recognized as State Historical Landmark #219.

Anti-Fat Canyon. Stephenson suggests that this canyon (later the site of the Buffalo Ranch) may have been named by Irvine Ranch employees. Meadows (1966:21) explains that "Anti-fat was a weight-reducing compound that was highly advertised years ago." He wonders if the name was "a misinterpretation of some surveyor's notes where the canyon was probably called Mule Fat..., the common name of a tall, brushy plant that was abundant in the canyon."

Arch Beach. A community laid out in 1887 by "Nate" Brooks, Hubbard Goff, and H.F. Stafford on Brooks' 1876 homestead below Laguna Beach. It had its own post office from 1889 to 1894. Goff built a hotel here at the end of what is now Rockledge Road. In 1897, it was cut in thirds and moved up to Laguna Beach to become part of the original Hotel Laguna.

Arches, The. Popular name for the area where Newport Boulevard crosses the Coast Highway in Newport Beach. It was named for a 1920s gas station and cafe located on the highway, which featured Mediterranean-style architecture, complete with arches. The Arches restaurant occupies the site today.

Artesia Street. A Mexican-American neighborhood in west Santa Ana, centered around Raitt Street, which was formerly known as Artesia Street. The Raitt family were dairy farmers who settled here in the 1890s.

Atwood. During the Boom days of the 1880s, a townsite known as Richfield was laid out here along the Santa Fe Railroad. The area faded with the Boom, but was revived around 1920 after oil was discovered in the area. The community was renamed Atwood "in honor of W.J. Atwood, purchasing agent of the Chanslor-Canfield Midway Oil Company, which had extensive holdings in the locality" (Meadows, 1966:23). A post office was established in 1924, and remains in operation, even though the community voted to annex to Placentia in 1970.

B

Back Bay. Popular name for the Upper Newport Bay. Backbay Drive winds along its eastern edge.

Baker Canyon. A tributary of Santiago Canyon, named for Charles Baker (d. 1919), a beekeeper who patented a homestead in this area in 1899. The names of Baker Canyon and Hall Canyon have been switched on modern maps.

Balboa. Once a separate town, founded in 1905, and now a part of the City of Newport Beach. "The name Balboa was suggested by E.J. Louis, at that time vice-counsel from Peru in Los Angeles." (Meadows, 1966:23). Vasco Núñez de Balboa (1475-1519) was a Spanish explorer, and the first European to cross Panama and see the Pacific Ocean. A post office opened in 1907 and survives as a station of Newport Beach. The Pacific Electric Railroad reached Balboa on July 4, 1906, and served the community until 1940. At one time, the entire city of Newport Beach considered changing its name to Balboa. **Balboa Island**. Developed beginning in 1906 by W.S. Collins, who had the bay dredged to build up the mudflats here. The original post office on the island was known as Balisle (1927-28) because the Post Office Department insisted on a one-word name, but they eventually agreed to accept Balboa Island. The eastern tip of the island — separated by a canal — was once called Channel Isle, but today is commonly known as Little Island. **Balboa Peninsula**. Before Balboa was founded, the peninsula was sometimes spoken of as The Spit. After the jetty was built, surfers dubbed the tip of the peninsula The Wedge. Today the neighborhood is usually called Peninsula Point.

Barber City. A more or less triangular townsite laid out in 1924 and named for Long Beach real estate agent Henry Barber. It was located south of Westminster Avenue, near Springdale Street. The community became part of the City of Westminster when it incorporated in 1957, but the name is still sometimes heard.

Barham Ranch. Originally know as the Squires Ranch, after E.W. Squires, a Southern California resident since the mid-1850s, who settled here in 1870. J.F. Barham owned the land for just a few years, but it was his name that became attached to the area. The ranch was purchased by the Serrano and Carpenter water companies in 1883, which only wanted it for its water rights on the Santiago Creek. For much of the early 20th century it was known as the Water Ranch, and the land was rented out for grazing. The Serrano Irrigation District owned an interest in the land until 2000. It has recently been sold to the County of Orange to be preserved as open space.

Barton Mound. Los Angeles County Sheriff James Barton and three of his men were ambushed and murdered here by the bandit Juan Flores and his gang in 1857. Flores later paid for his crimes at the end of a rope. The spot is now State Historical Landmark #218, located southeast of the 405 Freeway and Highway 133. *See* **Flores Peak** and **Presita Canyon**.

Bastanchury. Around 1870, Domingo Bastanchury (1836-1909) established a sheep ranch here in the hills between Fullerton and La Habra. Eventually he acquired some 6,000 acres. After his death, his wife and sons founded the Bastanchury Ranch Company, and went from sheep grazing to oranges, planting 3,000 acres of citrus. It was said to be the largest citrus ranch in the world. The Pacific Electric built a branch line across the ranch in 1917 and named their station here Bastanchury. But the ranch did not survive the depression of the 1930s, and the Bastanchurys lost the property. *See* **Sunny Hills**.

Bay City. The original name for Seal Beach. The townsite was laid out in 1903 by Phil Stanton and others, between Alamitos and Anaheim bays. A post office opened in 1904, and the school district was established in 1906. The community was renamed Seal Beach in 1913. The post office was changed in 1914, but the Bay City School District was not renamed until 1928.

Bay Island. The only natural island in Newport Harbor. "In 1903 Rufus Sanborn bought the island and with friends incorporated the Bay Island Club. The island was divided into twenty-four parcels, each parcel carrying one share in the club which held title to the land. Members built homes as personal property around the periphery of the island. A club house, since removed, was built in the center. The property is still controlled by the Bay Island Club" (Meadows, 1966:25). Because actress Helena Modjeska lived her last years on the island, it was sometimes called Modjeska Island after her death in 1909.

Bay Shores. Originally a vacation campground known as Bay Shore Camp, which opened in 1928. In 1937 The Irvine Company laid out a private community adjoining it on the shores of Newport Bay.

Bay View. A forgotten early school district, organized around 1878, and active for only a few years before it was annexed to the Fountain Valley district in 1886. The bay in view was obviously somewhere along the upper Orange County coast.

Beacon Bay. An upscale residential tract on Newport Bay, developed by longtime Newport Harbor booster Joseph Beek beginning in 1939.

Beanville. A farming community that grew up on the Irvine Ranch in the 1890s, east of Old Town Irvine. It was also sometimes known as Bean Town (the beans in question were limas). The Irvine Ranch was a major producer of lima beans in the first half of the 20th century. By 1911, there were already 14,000 acres of lima beans on the ranch.

Bear Flat. "There must be a Bear Flat in every county in California," Don Meadows observes (1966:25), and in fact Erwin Gudde counted about 500 "bear" place names up and down the state (1998:29). Our Bear Flat is located near Modjeska Peak, at the head of what the old timers called Bear Canyon, which is now called Halfway Canyon on maps, "thanks to indifferent cartographers," Jim Sleeper complains (1976:170). The name dates back to 1875, when famed hunter Jonathan Watson killed a bear here after it nearly got him first and badly mauled his companion.

Bedford Peak. Named for Thomas Bedford, who ran the former Butterfield stage station in Temescal Canyon on the east side of the mountains from 1869 to 1872. The name was originally applied to a nearby canyon, but had worked its way up to the peak by 1892.

Bed Rock Canyon. A narrow, rocky stretch of the Santa Ana River, below the mouth of Coal Canyon near the county line. The name was already in use in 1877; in 1884 it was made the measuring point for dividing irrigation water between the Anaheim Union Water Company and the Santa Ana Valley Irrigation Company.

Bell Canyon (sometimes Belle Canyon in the early days). "Along ...[San Juan] canyon are a number of branches, the most interesting of which perhaps is Bell canyon. This canyon was known in Mexican days as Cañada de la Campana, the Canyon of the Bell, because of a boulder located in the canyon. This rock when pounded gave forth a peal that filled the canyon" (Stephenson, 1931:50-51). In 1936 the famed boulder was moved to the courtyard of the Bowers Museum where it can still be seen.

Benedict. A townsite laid out in 1905 along the Pacific Electric tracks at Beach Boulevard and Katella Avenue. Some old timers claimed that a local rancher had allowed the PE a free right-of-way across his land on the promise that the company would build a depot there. But when they did not, he said the PE were a bunch of traitors, and so he laid out his own townsite named after Benedict Arnold, the famous Revolutionary War turncoat. In fact, it was the Pacific Electric Land Company itself which laid out the townsite, and the Benedict name first appears in 1896 as the name of a station on the Southern Pacific branch line to Los Alamitos. The station may have been named after W.E. Benedict, who was the SP's passenger agent in San Francisco around that time. The area later became part of the City of Stanton.

Berry. A Pacific Electric stop in Brea, where the tracks crossed Berry Street. Both were named for Truman Berry, a prominent early rancher.

Berrydale. An early 1900s farming community, located near Fairview Street and Seventeenth Street in what is now Garden Grove. Strawberries were the source of its name, said to have been the creation of local rancher D.W. McDannald, Orange County's publicity agent in the early 1900s. He also lobbied the "muck-a-mucks" of the Pacific Electric to change the name of their nearby Buaro station to Berrydale. "'Buaro' falls upon the ear like the sound of a long overdue bill...," he wrote. "While 'Berrydale' suggests a banquet, with good cheer in abundance and berries and cream on the half shell" (*Register*, April 20, 1909).

Big Canyon. Stephenson suggests this wide canyon was named by employees of the Irvine Ranch. Part of the site of the 1953 Boy Scout Jamboree (which gave its name to Jamboree Road), in 1971 the Big Canyon Country Club opened here, with its golf course and custom homes.

Bixby Hills. An earlier name for the ridge where Anaheim Hills is now located. After the Irvines and the O'Neills, the Bixby family probably owned more of Orange County than any other early ranching family — though their holdings were spread across the county, rather than in one single ranch. By the 1880s, the Jotham Bixby Company owned thousands of acres here. The land was used for grazing and farming. The Bixby Company also laid out the Cerro Villa and Peralta Hills tracts. By 1944 they had disposed of all their holdings. In 1987, as development increased on the south side of the hills, the City of Orange decided they did not want to use the name Anaheim Hills and voted to call the area the Nohl Hills, but that name quickly disappeared from sight.

Black Star Canyon. Known as Cañon de los Indios (Canyon of the Indians) in Mexican times, William Wolfskill led an attack on a group of Indians here in 1831. The Black Star Coal Mining Company opened a mine near the mouth of the canyon in 1877 and gave the canyon its present name. The mine operated off and on until the early 1900s.

Bloomfield. A portion of this school district was in Orange County when it was formed in 1889, but the schoolhouse was on the other side of Coyote Creek. The district was soon divided along the Los Angeles/Orange County line, with the local territory annexed to several other districts. But the name survives in Bloomfield Street on the western edge of the county.

Bluebird Canyon. A residential area in Laguna Beach, "it is the home of several writers and artists," Meadows (1966:28) notes. It was originally called Rimrock Canyon. After the 1932 Olympics, a Los Angeles entrepreneur moved a number of the tiny cottages from the Olympic Village into the upper canyon to create a rustic neighborhood.

Boca de la Playa. A Mexican rancho, granted to Emigdio Vejar in 1846, just two months before the United States captured California during the Mexican War. The name translates as "mouth of the beach." It was also sometimes called the Rancho Sacramento. When officially surveyed, it was found to contain 6,607 acres — quite small for a California rancho. Vejar sold the rancho to Juan Ávila in 1860, and it passed to his son-in-law, Pablo Pryor, in 1864. After his death in 1878, it was sold to Marcos Forster. Capistrano Beach and portions of San Clemente now occupy the old rancho.

Bolero Peak. A small peak west of the mouth of Modjeska Canyon. A U.S. Forest Service fire lookout was located here for many years; it was finally razed in 1989. The name in Spanish can mean a liar or a braggart. Terry Stephenson wrote that "Bolero" was the nickname of a Mexican *vaquero* in the mid-19th century, who was indeed a braggart. He later got his comeuppance near the little peak and the name stuck. "I've always thought Terry did more justice to the 'Bolero' story than it deserved," Jim Sleeper notes. "The name Bolero on maps seems not to pre-date 1923" (1976:163). Meadows suggests that "Perhaps the name is a corruption of the Spanish verb *velar* meaning 'to watch over'" (1966:28).

Bolsa. A little cross-roads hamlet near Bolsa Avenue and Brookhurst Street that took its name from the Rancho Las Bolsas. American settlers began arriving in the area in the 1860s, and in 1871 the Bolsa Grande School District was formed. The name was shortened to Bolsa in 1894, and the district was annexed to Garden Grove in 1929. Bolsa had its own post office at two different times, from 1886 to 1891, and again from 1895 to 1904. In 1887, an unsuccessful townsite known as Crestline was laid out here. **Bolsa Chica**. An 8,100-acre rancho carved out of the Rancho Las Bolsas in 1841 and granted to Joaquín Ruíz. It was later acquired by Abel Stearns. In the early 1900s, the Bolsa Chica Gun Club, the best-known of Orange County's many hunting clubs, shot ducks on the marshes here. A long strip of sand along the coast here was known as Tin Can Beach before it became a state park in 1960. A little further inland, the Bolsa Chica Wetlands have been a source of continuing friction between developers, environmentalists, and others for decades.

Bommer Canyon. The cattle headquarters for the Irvine Ranch for many years. The name appears on maps as early as the 1940s, though no one seems quite clear on its origin. Some of the old cowboys on the Irvine Ranch thought it might be a corruption of "bummer" — cowboy slang for a calf that has lost its mother. Today the site is used as a recreation area for barbecues, company picnics and the like.

Bonita Canyon. The name for this creek and canyon on the Irvine Ranch (meaning "pretty" in Spanish) has been in use since at least the 1910s.

Borrego Canyon. The name is Spanish for "yearling lamb." The canyon is located on the edge of the Irvine Ranch, which was operated as a sheep ranch in the 1860s and '70s.

Borromeo. A failed townsite, laid out in 1901 in what is now Placentia. It was named for Caroline Borromeo Polhemus, the wife of John K. Tuffree, who laid out the tract. Bastanchury Road in Placentia was once known as Borromeo Road.

Boulevard Gardens. In 1923, a townsite dubbed Aldrich was laid out here at the southwest corner of Beach Boulevard and Edinger Avenue. It was reborn a year later as Boulevard Gardens (though there is still an Aldrich Avenue here). Beach Boulevard was known as Huntington Beach Boulevard in those days, but the name was often shortened to just "the Boulevard." The tract offered larger lots, "Where you can have your orchard, chickens, rabbits, garden, fruit, flowers, lawns and shade" (*Huntington Beach News*, Feb. 29. 1924). The community never grew very large, and the area was annexed to the City of Huntington Beach in 1957.

Brea. In 1903, a townsite known as Randolph was laid out below the mouth of Brea Canyon. It didn't get very far, but in 1911 it was revived as Brea. A post office opened in 1912, and the community incorporated in 1917. For many years it was one of the centers of the oil industry in Orange County. The word *brea* is Spanish for "tar." **Brea Canyon**. A natural pass between the Puente and Chino hills. Asphaltum (dried oil and soil) and tar seeps were once common here, and the rancheros gathered the *brea* to help waterproof the roofs of their adobes. The name was first applied to the canyon in the 1840s, if not before. The first local oil explorations were launched here in the mid-1860s, but proved unsuccessful. Later oil companies had better luck.

Brookhurst. A freight station on the Southern Pacific's Santa Ana Branch at what became Brookhurst Avenue in Anaheim. Built in 1886, the station was removed in 1935. Hurst is Old English for a grove or thicket.

Browning. A Santa Fe station on Bryan Avenue, just southeast of Browning Avenue in Tustin. Meadows reports that it was named for Frank Browning, "who had 160 acres of nearby land on lease from the Irvine Company" (1966:30-31).

Buaro. A stop on Pacific Electric Railway on Harbor Boulevard near Westminster Avenue in what is now the City of Garden Grove. Part of what is now Harbor was once known as Buaro Road. There was also a Buaro voting precinct here in the 1910s and '20s. The name means buzzard in Spanish. *See* **Berrydale**.

Buck Gully. In use (as Buck Gulch) as early as 1926. "That is just another name, given possibly because somebody had good luck as a hunter thereabouts" (Stephenson, 1932:114). The canyon drains into the sea at Corona del Mar.

Buena Park. James A. Whitaker, a successful Chicago grocer, purchased 480 acres here in 1885 to start a stock ranch. When the Santa Fe was preparing to build through the area two years later, he was persuaded to launch a new townsite in cooperation with the Pacific Land Improvement Company — a development company controlled by Santa Fe officials. Several stories attempt to explain how the city got its name. Local historian Hub Chamberlin claimed that below the Los Coyotes adobe was once a "spring of good water and grass for animals. It had been called 'Plaza Buena' meaning 'good place' or 'good park.' It is probable that Buena Park got its name from that camping spot" (Chamberlin, 1971:7). Others have suggested that the tract was named after a Chicago suburb also known as Buena Park, where the Whitaker family once lived. The name also sounds a little like "real estate Spanish" — those hybrid names and curious translations selected for their romantic appeal. A little park with a fountain fed by an artesian well was touted as one of the attractions of the new town, and the new community was sometimes referred to simply as "the Park" in the local newspapers of the day. The City of Buena Park incorporated in 1953.

Buffalo Ranch. Properly the Newport Harbor Buffalo Ranch. Gene Clark operated this tourist attraction from 1954 to about 1960. It was located east of MacArthur Boulevard, below Bonita Canyon Drive. Architect William Pereira took over the buildings for a local office while his firm was developing the master plan for the Irvine Ranch. He called the spot Urbanus Square. Today, there is a Buffalo Hills Park in the area. *See* **Anti-Fat Canyon**.

Burruel Point. An earlier name for the Olive area, popular from the 1860s to the 1880s. Desiderio Burruel married Teodocio Yorba's daughter María, and by the late 1850s was the leading figure in the community. The Burruels lived in Teodocio's old adobe on the hill at Olive, and Desiderio had a store nearby. Later mapmakers shifted the name east to the top of Nohl Ranch; it appears on maps long after the community name had vanished.

Bushard. "A flag stop on the old Santa Ana-Huntington Beach line of the Pacific Electric Railway where it crossed Adams and Bushard streets in Huntington Beach. The stop was named for John B. Bushard, who farmed the surrounding territory" (Meadows, 1966:31). Passenger service on this line was abandoned in 1922, and the tracks removed some years later.

C

Cajon. A school district founded in 1874 to serve the Placentia area. The name was borrowed from the Rancho San Juan Cajón de Santa Ana. The district was renamed Placentia in 1878.

Cameo Shores. A 1950s Irvine Company development south of Corona del Mar along Newport Bay. A tract above it is known as Cameo Highlands.

Camp Rathke. During World War II, the Army occupied Irvine Park and the old Health Camp/Boy Scout camp adjoining it. In 1943 the camp was named in honor of Lt. George Rathke of Orange, who had been killed while on maneuvers earlier that spring. Two miles to the south, in Peters Canyon, a second military installation was known as Camp Commander.

Campo Colorado. Originally built in 1917 as a worker camp for employees of the La Habra Citrus Association. It was located south of the Union Pacific tracks near Monte Vista Street in La Habra. Many of the houses here were painted red in the old days, which gave the camp its name. It was also sometimes known as Red Camp. By the early 1970s, the community had faded away.

Campo Corona (Corona Camp). A Mexican-American community laid out around 1923 west of Campo Colorado. It was named for Charles Corona, who helped with sales in the 1920s. In 1980, the population in the area was estimated at about 600. A nearby park is known as Corona Park.

Campo Pomona (Pomona Camp). The worker camp for the Placentia Orange Growers Association, established around 1920 along South Balcom Avenue, near the Santa Fe tracks in Fullerton. Many of those early pickers came here from Pomona — hence the name.

Cañada de los Alisos. A Mexican rancho, originally granted to José Antonio Serrano in 1842 and enlarged in 1846. Still, by rancho standards, it was rather small — just a little over 10,000 acres. The name means "canyon of the sycamores" in Spanish. The Serrano family later lost the land to debt, and Dwight Whiting acquired most of it in the 1880s. One of the Serrano family adobes has been preserved at Heritage Hill in Lake Forest, and is now State Historical Landmark #199.

Cañon de Santa Ana. Bernardo Yorba's 13,300-acre rancho on the north side of the Santa Ana Canyon, granted in 1834. His home and rancho were also sometimes known as San Antonio or the Cañada de Santa Ana. The ruins of Yorba's large two-story adobe home stood until 1926, and the site is now State Historical Landmark #226.

Canyon Acres. A residential area east of Laguna Canyon Road. Canyon Acres was originally the name of the home of Harvey Hemenway, built here in the 1890s. Later the name spread to the canyon itself.

Capistrano Beach. This was the site of San Juan-by-the-Sea, a short-lived townsite from the Boom of the Eighties. The area was revived in 1925 as Capistrano Beach, but settlers were few. In 1928, Edward L. Doheny, Jr., the son of a rich Southland oil family, began promoting the community. But Doheny was murdered a few months later, and in 1931 the community was renamed **Doheny Park** in his honor (*see*). The Capistrano Beach name was revived in 1948, and the Doheny Park Post Office and the old Serra School District both adopted the name. Today, the community is a part of the City of Dana Point.

Carbon Canyon. The many black oil seeps rising out of the ground here gave the canyon its name, which was in use as early as 1900. Orange County's Carbon Canyon Regional Park opened here in 1975.

Carbondale. An 1878 mining town near the mouth of Silverado Canyon, on the flats near the Holtz Ranch. It was originally known as Harrisburg, after Tom Harris, who the owners of the property, the Southern Pacific Railroad, had placed in charge of the townsite. But the post office was named Carbondale (1881-84). Rather inferior coal was mined at several locations in the Santa Ana Mountains at that time. The site is now California State Historical Landmark #228.

Carlton. A failed townsite laid out in 1888 near Prospect Avenue and Imperial Highway in what is now Yorba Linda. It was surrounded by the Olinda Tract, and consisted of scores of tiny little lots. But the Boom of the Eighties had already burst when Carlton went on the market, and the town never went anywhere. In the 1920s, the Pacific Electric stop at Prospect Avenue was known as Carlton.

Caspers Wilderness Park. Part of the old Starr Ranch was sold for development in 1970 to the Macco Corporation. They soon got into financial trouble and lost the land. The northern end went to the Audubon Society, while the County of Orange bought 5,500 acres on the south which they opened as the Starr-Viejo Wilderness Park in 1974. Later that same year, the park was renamed for County Supervisor Ronald Caspers, who had mysteriously disappeared at sea that summer.

Celery. A short-lived station on the Southern Pacific's Smeltzer branch near Brookhurst Street and Pacific Coast Highway. Celery was the big new local crop at the time the Smeltzer branch was built in 1897, but eventually it faded away. *See* **Nago**.

Centralia. In the early 1870s, the Stearns Ranchos Company laid out a 480-acre tract southeast of Buena Park that they named Centralia. They hoped to sell the area for a "colony" development (like Westminster), but the plan failed, and the tract was never filed with the county. Enough settlers did move into the area to justify the founding of a Sunday School, a literary society, and eventually the Centralia School District, which was organized in 1875. The original district was very large, and several other districts were later carved out of it. What is now Crescent Avenue was once Centralia Road.

Cerro Villa Heights. A residential tract first subdivided in 1920 by the Jotham Bixby Company in what is now the northeastern part of the City of Villa Park. The developers translated its Spanish name as "hill home."

Chico. "A short-lived school district, organized in 1890 southwest of Westminster Avenue. The little schoolhouse was located on the west side of Springdale Avenue a half mile south of Westminster Boulevard" (Meadows, 1966:52). The area returned to the Westminster District in 1911. The name is probably a corruption from the Rancho Bolsa Chica.

Chino Hills. In the early 1800s, the Mission San Gabriel grazed cattle all across the northern end of Orange County. They called the area the Rancho Santa Ana. Later, they added Chino to the name to distinguish their rancho from the other Santa Ana ranchos nearby. In early, Spanish-speaking California, the name *chino* usually meant a curly haired man. It was said to be the nickname of one of the mission's *vaqueros*. In 1841, the eastern end of the old mission rancho, in what is now San Bernardino County, was granted to Antonio María Lugo as the Rancho Santa Ana del Chino. The Chino Hills State Park here was created in 1983, and includes parts of three counties — Orange, San Bernardino, and Riverside.

Ciénaga de las Ranas. Spanish for the "swamp of the frogs," a marshy area which once stretched from the top of Newport Bay north to the foothills. The name was in use as early as 1801. "This long, wide stretch of waterlogged country was covered with willows, tules, guatamotes, marshy ground and open water," Meadows explains. "During winter months it was a swamp that could not be crossed, even on horseback. Millions of tree frogs...lived in the swamp, and in the spring they joined their high-pitched voices into a mighty chorus that could be heard for miles. On dark nights riders on El Camino Real would keep their bearings by listening to the frogs" (1966:52).

City Garden Acres. A residential tract laid out in 1924 near the southeast corner of Los Alamitos Boulevard and Katella Avenue, just south of Los Alamitos. It was also sometimes shortened to just Garden Acres. Green Street, which still survives here, was named for Rush P. Green, the original tract agent.

Clair. A little post office established in 1895 near Magnolia and Cerritos avenues, in what is now Stanton. The post office closed in 1900, when rural free delivery began. The source of the name is unknown, and even the spelling varies. Around 1898, local Methodists built what was sometimes called the Clare Methodist Episcopal Church here. In 1920 the building was moved to Stanton where it was turned over to the Methodist Church's Latin American ministry. Later it served as a Catholic Church.

Cleveland National Forest. In 1893, 50,000 acres in the Santa Ana Mountains were set aside as the Trabuco Canyon Forest Reserve. In 1908, it was combined with the San Jacinto Forest Reserve to form the Cleveland National Forest, named in honor of former President Grover Cleveland, who died that same year.

Coal Canyon. Coal had been noted in the Santa Ana Canyon area as early as 1864, but there was no real development in the area until the Confidence Mine was staked here in 1876. Like most local mines, it was never a big producer.

Coast Royal. "In 1906 a man named Horace J. Pullen acquired an interest in some land halfway between Laguna Beach and Dana Point and without consulting the other owner laid out a subdivision he named Coast Royal. His partner, Miss Blanche Dolph, who was in Europe when he placed the property on the market, heard of his activities and filed suit to stop the project. Los Angeles newspapers branded Coast Royal a swindle, and the project died" (Meadows, 1966:53). The tract was located above Aliso Beach. It was revived in the early 1920s, and proved successful.

Collins Island. William S. Collins, the "inordinately handsome, polished and urbane ... playboy-developer" of Balboa Island (Felton, 1981:31, 35) built his home on this little island around 1906. He sold the island in 1915, and in 1938 it was purchased by actor James Cagney. During World War II, the Coast Guard leased the island from Cagney. Later the island was subdivided, and the Collins home was demolished.

Colonia Independencia. A Mexican-American community laid out in 1923 at the northwest corner of Katella Avenue and Gilbert Street, in what is still an unincorporated area between Anaheim and Stanton.

This was one of several tracts laid out about that time to cater to the county's growing Mexican-American population. In 1980, its population was estimated at 1,000.

Colonia Juárez. A Mexican-American community laid out in 1923 by Ashby Turner, a Santa Ana real estate developer. It is located south of Warner Avenue along Ward Street, just south of Mile Square Regional Park in Fountain Valley, It was named for 19th century Mexican President Benito Juárez, one of the most famous Mexican patriots. One of the original streets here (still extant) is known as Avenida Cinco de Mayo — probably the first "avenida" in Orange County.

Colonia La Paz. A Mexican-American community northeast of Westminster Avenue and Euclid Street, now in the City of Garden Grove. The tract was laid out in 1924, and soon became connected with Colonia Manzanillo. In Spanish, La Paz means "the peace."

Colonia Manzanillo. A Mexican-American community, laid out around 1925, southeast of Westminster Avenue and Euclid Street, now on the western edge of the City of Santa Ana. Manzanillo is the name of several communities in Mexico. In recent decades, the community has also sometimes been known as Colonia Diecisiete, or Colonia Seventeenth. Westminster Avenue was originally known as Seventeenth Street.

Commonwealth. A short-lived school district serving the area south and west of Placentia, north of the Santa Ana River. Formed in 1911, it was annexed to the Placentia-Richfield Union School District in 1920.

Coney Island. Once a popular name for the sandbars above Newport Dunes. Around 1930, it was proposed to build an elaborate waterfront recreation area here, but the idea never took off.

Cooks Corner. Andrew Jackson Cook settled here in the 1880s, and gave his name to the area. In the 1930s his son, Jack Cook, started a lunch counter and bar at the junction of El Toro Road and

Live Oak Canyon Road. Today, it is a popular watering hole for motorcyclists and other canyon travelers.

Corona del Mar. In 1904, developer George Hart took control of just over 700 acres above Rocky Point from The Irvine Company, and laid out a tract he called Corona del Mar (Spanish for "crown of the sea"). Limited access slowed the town's growth, and by 1915 there were just eight houses here. That same year, the F.D. Cornell Company took over the development of the tract, which they tried to rename Balboa Palisades. But the old name was too well established. The community was annexed to Newport Beach in 1923, and a post office was established three years later.

Costa Mesa. The original post office here was known as **Harper** (*see*) from 1909 to 1920. By then, the Harper family was long gone, and local residents held a contest to select a new name that was "harmonious, euphonious, and utilitarian" (*Newport News*, Feb. 20, 1920). Out of hundreds of entries, Alice Plummer made the winning suggestion (which means "coast tableland" in Spanish), and won the $25 prize. The post office was renamed that May, and the Harper-Fairview School District followed suit six years later. In 1953, after several years of rapid growth, the city was incorporated.

Coto de Caza. A gated residential community first developed in the 1970s. The Spanish name means a "hunting preserve," or a "place for hunting," and the original development featured a hunt club. The area had been part of the Ernest Bryant ranch since the late 1930s, and was sold to Macco Realty in 1963 for $5 million.

Cowan Heights. In 1944, Walter Cowan, an eccentric oilman, purchased 750 acres of the old Marcy Ranch in the foothills above Tustin. More than 180 acres of the land was planted to citrus, and the rest was used as grazing land. He named his new ranch Cowan Heights, and the name was carried over when the ranch was subdivided for residential development. Cowan died in 1973.

Coyote Creek. Much of Orange County's boundary with Los Angeles County follows Coyote Creek. The creek undoubtedly takes its name from the Rancho Los Coyotes, which it crosses. The name was already in use by the 1860s. **Coyote Hills**. Located near the northern boundary of the Rancho Los Coyotes, the Coyote Hills were known by that name by the 1870s. Later, they would prove to be one of Orange County's most productive oilfields. The little ridge is often divided as the East and West Coyote Hills.

Crawford Canyon. Named for real estate developer Francis E. Crawford. In 1910, he subdivided part of the surrounding hills as the El Modena Citrus Lands tract. The project seems to have been a financial failure for him, but the name survived. Another Crawford Canyon is located just over the county line in La Habra Heights.

Cristianitos Canyon (sometimes Christianitos). One of several local place names from the 1769 Portolá expedition still in use today. On July 22, 1769, the expedition's priests baptized two sick little girls in the Indian village here — the first baptisms in California. In Spanish and Mexican times the canyon was sometimes called the Cañada de los Bautismos.

Crow Canyon. The name is mentioned as early as 1919, and was seemingly old even then. Today the area is part of the Audubon Society's Starr Ranch Sanctuary.

Crystal Cove. A little seaside community established in the 1920s on land leased from The Irvine Company. It is said to have been named in 1927 by Elizabeth Wood because of the beauty of the spot. "The name is a misnomer," Meadows notes (1966:56), "for the beach at that place shows no indentation of any kind." Some 1,900 acres here, stretching up into the hills, were sold to the State of California in 1979 to form the Crystal Cove State Park. After much wrangling, the state agreed to preserve some of the old cottages as vacation rentals.

Culvers Corner. The three-way intersection of Culver Drive, Trabuco Road and old Highway 101 (now the route of Interstate 5). The junction was a well-known, though sometimes dangerous landmark on the Irvine Ranch for many years. It was known as The

Windmill in the late 19th century, when James Sleeper (the historian's grandfather) farmed here. Then Fred "Humpy" Culver — not to be confused with his brother "Gimpy" — took over the lease and built a substantial home at the corner. He died in 1918, but the name survived for many years.

Cypress. The Cypress School District was established in 1896, and a school was built near the northeast corner of Ball Road and Moody Street. Cypress trees were a popular ornamental plant in Southern California at the time, and their green boughs were often used for Christmas decorations. Like many outlying districts, the school name soon became attached to the community. The area was also sometimes called Waterville for the abundance of artesian wells here. When the Pacific Electric Railway arrived in 1905, they named their station Cypress, and a Cypress townsite was laid out that same year. The Cypress Post Office opened in 1927. In 1956, the area incorporated as Dairy City, but was quickly renamed Cypress.

Cypress Street. A Mexican-American barrio in downtown Orange which grew up near the packing houses along Cypress Street beginning in the 1910s. The old Cypress Street School here (built in 1931) is the last remaining building in the county to have been built as a segregated school.

D

Dairy City. The original name for the City of Cypress when it incorporated in 1956. The city was renamed a year later by a vote of 208 to 41. About that same time, Dairyland, and Dairy Valley (now Cerritos in Los Angeles County) were also incorporated. All three communities hoped to preserve their agricultural base against the rapid suburban growth of Southern California.

Dairyland. The original name of the city of La Palma when it incorporated in 1955. Jack DeVries, Dairyland's first mayor, later recalled that incorporation attorney Rodger Howell suggested the agricultural city's new name, based in part on Disneyland, which opened that same year. The first residential tracts finally arrived in 1965, the same year the city abandoned its original name.

Dalewood. A 1940s residential area near Garden Grove Boulevard and Dale Avenue, now a part of the City of Garden Grove. Lester Dale, Stanton's constable in 1915-16, may have been the source of the street name.

Dana Point (headlands). *Two Years Before the Mast*, Richard Henry Dana's classic account of the hide trade along the California coast, was a bestseller in the 1840s, and the first account that many Americans read of the far-off land of California. One of Dana's anchorages was off "a small cove or bight, which gave us, at high tide, a few square feet of sand-beach between the sea and the bottom of the hill." Here, they picked up hides from the Mission San Juan Capistrano and surrounding ranchos. By the 1870s, people had begun calling the headlands here Dana's Point or Dana Point. Other early maps label it San Juan Point. But according to local historian Doris Walker, the actual point where the men pitched the hides down to the beach was more likely a smaller one, just east of the headlands, that was later cut away when Dana Point Harbor was built (Walker, 1987:77). **Dana Point** (city). The first subdivision here was called Dana Heights. It was laid out in 1888 above the cove and out onto the headlands, but failed with the collapse of the real estate Boom. The Dana Point tract was laid out in 1924, but also faltered. Then in 1926, developer Sidney Woodruff (whose "Hollywoodland" tract is forever famous for its hillside sign) bought 1,200 acres here and started over. The new Dana Point tract went on the market January 15, 1927, and once the Pacific Coast Highway reached the area in 1929, its future was assured. The City of Dana Point (including Capistrano Beach and Monarch Bay) was incorporated in 1989. **Dana Point Harbor**. In the 1940s, planning began for a man-made harbor in Capistrano Bay. Surfers called the cove "Killer Dana." Construction on the harbor finally began in 1966. The breakwater was built first, sealed off, and then the entire harbor was pumped dry so it could be dredged. The east basin of the harbor opened in 1971, and the west basin followed five years later. There are berths for some 2,500 boats here.

Delhi. A community near Warner Avenue (originally Delhi Road), east of Main Street in what is now the City of Santa Ana. There was a Delhi School District here from 1879 to 1924, when it was re-named Hawthorne. But since there was already another Delhi, California, the post office here was known as Gloryetta (1915-36). The name is borrowed from Delhi, New York, the home of the McFadden family. There is no connection with the Indian city. James McFadden received 4,000 acres here in the partition of the Rancho Santiago de Santa Ana in 1868. The name here (and in New York) was always pronounced *dell-high*. The area was annexed to the City of Santa Ana in 1929.

Des Moines. A stop on the La Habra branch of the Pacific Electric Railway, where the tracks crossed Beach Boulevard. Index Orchards built their packing house here in 1914.

Diamond. A school district established in 1877 southwest of Santa Ana. The schoolhouse was originally located at Bristol Street and Edinger Avenue, but was later moved west to Edinger and Greenville Street. Eventually a community grew up around the school, which was known as Santa Ana Gardens. The school district merged with Santa Ana in 1949, but the Diamond School has survived. There is also a Diamond station of the Santa Ana Post Office here.

Disneyland. After an extensive search, film producer Walt Disney selected Anaheim as the site of his new theme park, and named it after himself. After a year of construction, Disneyland opened to the public on July 18, 1955, and Orange County's image was changed forever. In 2001, a second park, Disney's California Adventure, was added. Hotels, restaurants, and the Anaheim Convention Center are all nearby. The area around Disneyland is sometimes called the Anaheim Resort Area.

Doheny Park. An alternate name for Capistrano Beach from 1931 to 1948. Named for Edward L. Doheny Jr., who launched a community of Spanish-style homes on the bluff top here in 1928. The 62-acre Doheny State Beach, established in 1931, lies along the coast here.

Dove Canyon. Named for the birds, in the 19th century it was some-times known as La Cañada de la Paloma ("the canyon of the dove" in Spanish). Later it became part of the Starr Ranch. Today it is a gated residential community, which opened in 1989.

Dover Shores. A residential tract in Newport Beach, developed by Macco Realty in the early 1960s. It was named for the "Dover-like" cliffs of the Back Bay.

Dyer. "The end of a branch line of the Santa Ana-Huntington Beach Pacific Electric Railway that serviced the Santa Ana Cooperative Sugar Company on Dyer Road, south of Santa Ana" (Meadows, 1966:58). Named for Ebenezer H. Dyer, the first successful sugar beet grower in California. The sugar beet processing plant here was built in 1912, and was bought out by Holly Sugar in 1917. It was the last beet sugar plant in the county, still in operation in the 1980s (older residents will remember the thick, musty aroma). The build-ing was razed in 1983 and a hotel was built on the site.

E

Earlham. The original name for the post office in El Modena (1887-88), selected when postal officials decided the name Modena might be confused with the town of Madera, in Northern California. Many of the early settlers in the area were Midwestern Quakers, so they selected the name of the well-known Quaker college in Earlham, Indiana instead. In 1888 the post office was renamed El Modena.

East Bluff. A residential tract, first developed in 1962 on the east-ern bluffs of the Back Bay in Newport Beach.

East Lake (East Lake Village). An 860-acre residential area in Yorba Linda, developed in the late 1970s around a man-made lake of the same name.

East Newport. A community laid out in 1904 along Balboa Boule-vard, at Island Avenue, between Newport Beach and Balboa. It is now one of the many communities that now make up the City of Newport Beach.

El Modena. Originally known as Modena when it was founded in 1886, the community was named after a town in Italy, which was mentioned in a popular poem of the day. But the first post office here was named **Earlham** (*see*), after postal officials refused the original name. In 1888, a Spanish "El" was added to Modena, the post office was renamed, and everyone seemed satisfied. That is, until 1910, when some linguistic purist pressured the post office department to "correct" the name to El Modeno. Most local residents never adopted the "o" spelling, and the historic name was officially restored in 1970. Beginning in the 1910s, a large Mexican-American community grew up here. Today, much of the area is part of the City of Orange. Before El Modena was founded, the area was generally known as the Mesa. The rise up to the Mesa is still visible at Esplanade Street. The area below the Mesa, closer to the Santiago Creek, was referred to as the Gravel, for its rocky soil. **El Modena Grade**. In 1892, Chapman Avenue was extended up over the hills east of El Modena, creating a steep shortcut to the Picnic Grounds that later became Irvine Park. The road was first paved around 1920.

El Refugio. The name of José Sepúlveda's adobe residence in what is now Santa Ana. Stephenson says it was on Willitts Street. Meadows places it a little to the north near Myrtle Street and Raitt Street. "The first portion was built prior to 1846 by Domingo Yorba, the southern extension was added by Sepúlveda in 1860. In March 1871 fire destroyed parts of the building and in 1876 the whole structure was leveled to the ground. El Refugio was famous for its hospitality, and was the scene of many weddings, fiestas, barbecues, etc." (Meadows, 1966:118).

El Toro. Spanish for "the bull," the name was in use as early as 1838, when hundreds of cattle roamed the area. Still, legends persist — "There is an old, old story that a devout padre, by the holding up of his hands and a prayer to God, stayed the charge of a mad bull, and the place was called El Toro" (Stephenson, 1931:50). Stephenson credits Judge Richard Egan of San Juan Capistrano with giving the name to the Santa Fe station here in 1887. The local townsite was initially known as Aliso City, but the El Toro name proved stronger. The El Toro Post Office opened in 1888, and the El Toro School District was organized two years later. El Toro remained a quiet little farming community until the 1960s, when the first tract houses appeared. In 1963, there was a move to rename the community Laguna North. Today it is part of the City of Lake Forest — though the El Toro Post Office has survived. **El Toro Marine Base**. Properly the United States Marine Corps Air Station at El Toro, it was established in 1942 on some of the best farmland on the Irvine Ranch. It eventually grew to more than 4,600 acres. The base was decommissioned in 1999 and purchased at auction by the Lennar Corp. in 2005 for nearly $650 million. Planning is currently underway for the commercial, industrial, and residential development of the area — along with a "great park" on a portion of the old base. **El Toro Y**. The popular name for the junction of the Santa Ana (5) and San Diego (405) freeways, just south of the El Toro Marine base in Irvine. The freeways met in 1968, and the name was made popular by traffic reporters in the 1980s. Now it is even used by government agencies in official publications. *See* **Orange Crush**.

Emerald Bay. A residential community along the Laguna coast. The cove was originally called Green Bay. Doris Bathgate, whose father ran an auto camp at the cove in the 1920s, is credited with suggesting the name Emerald Bay for its sparkling green waters. The first residential tracts here followed the completion of the Coast Highway through the area in the late 1920s. Originally most of the homes were only used as summer vacation spots. As late as 1945, there were still only about 40 year-round residents. The canyon that drains into the bay has been known as Emerald Canyon since at least the 1960s.

Emery Lease. In 1894, Frank Emery purchased a large ranch that included the West Coyote Hills. In 1912, the Standard Oil Company leased 80 acres up in the hills for oil exploration, and a little worker camp grew up here. During the first decades of the 20th century, worker camps were scattered across the oil leases in the northern part of the county. Some were home to just a few employees, while others had stores and churches and schools. Among the better known were the Associated Lease east of Brea, the Columbia Lease northwest of Olinda, and the G.P. (General Petroleum) Lease. As better transportation became available, workers were able to move off the leases and live in town, and by World War II the camps had largely faded.

Encyclopedia Lots. In 1915, a Midwestern publisher purchased several small subdivisions north of Huntington Beach on both sides of Ellis Avenue, between Edwards and Goldenwest streets. Scores of these tiny little lots were given away as a premium to purchasers of an encyclopedia series — often to out-of-state buyers who never even saw their supposed beachfront lots. "These were the worst tracts that could be found...back in the country on steep hillsides and in deep ravines" (Talbert, 1952:106-07). Then in 1922, oil was discovered underneath them, the lots suddenly became valuable, and "legal proceedings came thick and fast." (1952:108). The rights and royalties of these lots were a tangled mess for decades, but a group of local investors, led by County Supervisor Tom Talbert, managed to buy up a number of the lots, and over the next 30 years "netted...about a quarter of a million dollars," he recalled (1952:107-08).

Esperanza. A freight stop on the Santa Fe Railroad in the Santa Ana Canyon, named for the daughter of Prudencio Yorba, who died around 1870, at age 15. Yorba named his ranch for his daughter soon after her death, and the railroad later adopted the name. The siding was located along Esperanza Road, near Yorba Linda Boulevard. By the 1920s, a small community had grown up in the area.

Evergreen. A school district, a portion of which was in northern Orange County when the county was formed in 1889, although the schoolhouse was located in East Whittier. The local portion was annexed to the Orangethorpe School District a year later.

F

Fairhaven. A failed 1875 townsite northwest of Fairhaven Avenue and Esplanade Street in what is now the City of Orange. Rev. H.H. Messenger laid out the townsite as a temperance colony for his Episcopalian brethren. "Enraptured by the warm climate, he projected an agricultural community and planted thousands of banana and pineapple plants. Lack of water, Santa Ana winds, and shallow soil were factors not considered, and after two years of effort the undertaking was abandoned" (Meadows, 1966:61). The street, and later the cemetery (founded in 1911) perpetuate its name. *See* **Messenger Hill**.

Fairview (colony). Two local communities have carried this name. The first — sometimes called the Fairview Colony — was located southwest of Anaheim, near where Disneyland now stands. The Fairview School District was established here in 1869, and the community retained its identity on into the 1880s, even though it never developed into a town.

Fairview (town). Just about the time the first Fairview was fading, a new boom town of Fairview was laid out south of Santa Ana, in what is now Costa Mesa. Founded in 1887, it got a post office in 1888 and a school district a year later. The Fairview townsite was centered around Harbor Boulevard and Adams Avenue. The inevitable tourist hotel was two blocks to the north. Paul Knauff, a Santa Ana banker, is said to have suggested the name. Visiting the site he exclaimed, "Look at the beautiful view. Let's call the town Fairview!" (Miller, 1976:13). But the Boom soon collapsed, and Fairview went with it. In 1891 the hotel was moved to some hot mineral springs on what is now the Orange Coast College campus. The post office closed in 1903, and the school district merged with Harper in 1915. Then in 1918, the San Jacinto Earthquake cut off the flow of the hot springs, and old hotel was torn down two years later.

Falls Canyon. A small tributary of Trabuco Canyon, just west of Holy Jim Canyon. It features several small, seasonal waterfalls.

Featherly Regional Park. Orange County's third regional park, and the first of many to be named for a former County Supervisor. Known as Sycamore Flat Regional Park during its planning stages, it was named for longtime County Supervisor C.M. (Cye) Featherly when it opened in 1970.

Fishermans Cove. The Laguna coast is dotted with named coves — even if some of them hardly make a dent in the coastline. Fishermans Cove is one of the oldest names. It was already in use in 1895. Cowards Cove was in use by 1905 (certainly a good story must lay behind that name). Divers Cove appears by the 1920s and is still a popular destination for scuba divers today. Then there was Cape Cove, Reef Cove, Shaws Cove, Shelter Cove, and others.

Five Points. A popular name for the intersection of Beach Boulevard, Main Street, and Ellis Avenue, which seems to date back to the oil boom of the 1920s, when several wildcat wells were drilled here. The area was annexed to the City of Huntington Beach in 1957 and became the first major shopping district outside of the old downtown area. There is another Five Points in Anaheim, where Center Street, Lincoln Avenue, and West Street converge.

Floral Park. A residential tract in north Santa Ana, laid out in the 1920s. There was a Floral Park station of the Santa Ana Post Office here from 1953 to 1969.

Flores Peak. A small rise on the ridge between Harding and Modjeska Canyon, it was named for the bandit Juan Flores, whose gang shot up San Juan Capistrano in 1857 and killed Los Angeles County Sheriff James Barton. Flores managed to outfox his pursuers, making his escape along this ridge. He was later captured and hanged for his crimes. Over the years, there have been many buried treasure stories associated with the peak. It is now recognized as State Historical Landmark #225. *See* **Barton Mound** and **Presita Canyon**.

Foothill Ranch. The first homes in this 2,740-acre planned community went on sale in 1991. Its location in the foothills above the Saddleback Valley may have inspired the name. In 2000, it became a part of the City of Lake Forest.

Forest of Arden. The summer home of Shakespearean actress Helena Modjeska, built in 1888 in the canyon that now bears her name. The Forest of Arden was one of the settings in Shakespeare's "As You Like It." As Modjeska explained, "like the Forest of Arden in 'As You Like It,' everything that Shakespeare speaks of was on the spot, — oak trees, running brooks, palms, snakes, and even lions — of course California lions — really pumas" (Friis, 1965:73). Modjeska sold the property in 1906. Today it is an Orange County historic park, and one of the county's few National Historic Landmarks.

Forster. A short-lived post office at San Juan-By-The-Sea (1888-1891), established after that name was judged too long by postal officials. Not to be confused with the earlier Forster Post Office (1879-1883) at Forster City, which was located just below the mouth of San Onofre Creek in San Diego County. Both post offices were named for Juan Forster (1814-1882), an Englishman who settled in California in 1833 and eventually owned the vast Santa Margarita Ranch (now Camp Pendleton), along with the ranchos Trabuco and Mission Viejo in Orange County. Forster City did not survive Forster's death. San Juan-By-The-Sea is now Capistrano Beach.

Fountain Valley. The name was in use as early as 1875, when a promotional pamphlet explained, "The name Fountain Valley was applied when it was discovered that a pipe driven into the ground would produce an abundance of artesian water" (Meadows, 1966:63). The original Fountain Valley School District was formed in 1876, but lapsed in 1890. It was re-organized in 1898. When the community applied for a post office in 1899, the two-word name was refused, and **Talbert** (*see*) was substituted. The City of Fountain Valley was incorporated in 1957 when the area was still largely agricultural. A Fountain Valley Post Office finally opened as a branch of Santa Ana in 1958.

Fourth Crossing. Old timers heading up the Santiago Creek into the Santa Ana Mountains made their first crossing in what is now Irvine Park, then three more before the canyon opened up into Sycamore Flat. The Fourth Crossing, near Mancow Rock, was a popular camping spot. It disappeared under the waters of Irvine Lake when the dam was completed in 1931.

Frances. A railroad stop on the Venta spur line of the Santa Fe, near Yale and Bryan avenues in Irvine. The Frances Citrus packing house operated here from 1916 to 1971. Both the siding and the packing house were named for Frances Anita Plum, the first wife of James Irvine Jr., who died in 1909.

Freeway Park. A 1946 residential tract on La Palma Avenue, between Gilbert and Brookhurst streets. It lay along the proposed route of the Santa Ana Freeway. The community is now a part of Anaheim, but at least one local business still uses the old name.

Fremont Canyon. Originally known as Horca Canyon (Spanish for "choked") because of its narrow entrance, then as Sierra Canyon, after nearby Sierra Peak, and finally as Fremont Canyon. "John Charles Frémont had nothing to do with the beautiful canyon. In the early 1870s a man named Smith was in charge of a band of sheep that grazed in the upper canyon. Smith had campaigned with Frémont and talked so much of his old boss that he was given the nickname of 'Fremont.' The canyon thus acquired its official name" (Meadows, 1966:64-65). The name was in use by the 1880s.

French Hill. A little peak (426') north of the San Joaquin Hills in what is now Turtle Rock. It was named for C.E. French (1841-1914), general manager of the Irvine ranch from 1871 to 1878. Later a well-known Santa Ana businessman, French is credited with helping to move the ranch from grazing into farming during his tenure there.

Fruitland. A failed townsite from the Boom of the Eighties, located in South Santa Ana, southwest of Greenville Street and Warner Avenue. The townsite was never officially recorded and the community never developed.

Fuller Park — *see* **Lansdowne.**

Fullerton. The city was founded in 1887 by George and Edward Amerige in partnership with the Pacific Land Improvement Company (a development company controlled by stockholders in the Santa Fe Railroad). The community was named for George H.

Fullerton (1853-1929), the president of the Pacific Land Improvement Company, and the right-of-way agent for the Santa Fe. The Ameriges negotiated with Fullerton to bring the Santa Fe to their proposed tract, offering the necessary right-of-way and an interest in the property. Then they sweetened the deal by naming the town after him — though Fullerton's son later claimed his father really did not want the honor. In any case, Edward Amerige later recalled that by the time the first trains arrived in 1888, Fullerton had been "dispossessed of his title and interest" in the Santa Fe, so the railroad named their station here La Habra. "[B]ut opposition to the change in the name was so great that the original name was restored," Amerige wrote (Ziebell, 1994:50). A post office and school district were both established in 1888, and the city was incorporated in 1904. The Ameriges' original tract office still stands in Amerige Park.

G

Gabino Canyon. The name is colloquial Spanish for "sea gull" (properly, *gaviota*), and was also sometimes spelled Gavino. Current plans call for the area to be preserved as open space.

Galivan. Don Meadows originally assumed the name of this Santa Fe Railroad siding north of San Juan Capistrano near Oso Parkway was a corruption of the Spanish word *gavilan* or "sparrow hawk." Later he learned that it was "named for J.B. Galivan of Los Angeles. He was trainmaster for the Santa Fe Railroad when the line was built in 1888" (Meadows, 1996:5).

Garden Acres. A small residential area near Garden Grove Boulevard and Magnolia Street. It is now a part of the City of Garden Grove. *See* **City Garden Acres**.

Garden Grove. Settlers began arriving here in the late 1860s, and the name was first attached to the local school district in 1875. Alonzo Cook is usually credited with its selection. Nannie Price, a pioneer of 1874, recalled, "Some objected, thought it was not appropriate, as there was nothing that could be called a tree in the whole district, but Mr. Cook said: 'We'll make it appropriate by planting trees and making it beautiful'" (Armor, 1921:392). In 1876, Cook and Converse Howe laid out the Garden Grove townsite, and the first store, along with a post office, opened a year later. After nearly 40 years of debate and failed elections, the city finally incorporated in 1956. At that time, Garden Grove was considered one of the fastest-growing communities in the United States.

Gilman Peak. For many years a forest fire lookout was located on this little peak north of Yorba Linda in the Chino Hills. Don Meadows originally thought that it was named for citrus pioneer Richard H. Gilman, but later learned that it was named for Herbert Gilman, a member of the State Forestry Board, who died in 1935.

Gloryetta. The name of the post office at Delhi, which opened in June, 1915. Prior to that, the post office had been briefly known as **Harbor** (*see*). Perhaps the name is a gringo spelling of the Spanish word *glorieta*, meaning a small square where several streets meet. By the 1930s, Delhians got their mail on rural free delivery, and did most of their post office business in Santa Ana. During its last ten days of existence, the Gloryetta Post Office grossed a whopping 42¢. It was closed in April, 1936.

Gobernadora Canyon. Both Stephenson and Meadows agree that the name comes from the Spanish name for creosote bush. The name was already in common use in the 1850s. Today Coto de Caza occupies the top of the canyon.

Goff Island — *see* **Treasure Island**.

Gopher City. In 1935, the Alpha-Beta Company established a meat packing plant near Wintersburg to supply their growing chain of supermarkets. Many of the employees lived in housing on the north side of the plant. Officially known as the Beach Packing Plant, both the housing area and the packing plant became jokingly known as Gopher City, due to the prevalence of those burrowing rodents. There was also once an area known as Gopher City in what is now the City of La Palma.

Gospel Swamp. A well-known name in the late 19th century, it originally referred to the marshy lands below McFadden Avenue, south of Santa Ana, but it later spread west across Fountain Valley towards Huntington Beach. Walter Tedford, son of the first Anglo settler here, later recalled that the name was coined by George Lynch after listening to a sermon by Rev. Isaac Hickey, another early settler. "George was quite a critic and made many comments about the happenings in the community," Tedford wrote. "The name struck the boys as being a good one and of course the news spread and the name was universally adopted" (Tedford, 1931:91). The name was already in common use in 1873 when the *Los Angeles Star* noted, "The swamp was originally settled by a number of families, among whom were more than the usual proportion of preachers, so the community were remarkable for their piety and church-going. Hence the name of the settlement" (April 9, 1873). The city folk called their country cousins down in Gospel Swamp the "Swamp Angels." *See* **Old Newport** and **Republican Bend**.

Green River. A 1920s cabin resort on the south side of the Santa Ana River, just over the line into Riverside County. In 1948, the weeklong Green River fire started here and burned 47,000 acres across the Santa Ana Mountains — making it one of the largest fires in Orange County's history. The resort was lost to the freeway in the 1960s, but the name survives in a road and a golf course, which opened in 1959.

Greenville. Around 1915, Greenville began to replace the name **Old Newport** (*see*) for the farmlands south of Santa Ana. "Its name is especially appropriate, for the area is one vast expanse of unbroken green" (*Los Angeles Times*, Dec. 18, 1927). The Pacific Electric station at Greenville was located at Greenville Street and Alton Avenue, where the old lima bean warehouse still stands. The Greenville School was about the last one-room schoolhouse in Orange County when it closed in 1961. By the 1970s, some people were calling the area Griset Park, after one of the longtime local farming families, but the name never really caught on.

Gypsum Canyon. Gypsum was mined here on the south side of the Santa Ana Canyon for a few years in the late 19th century, giving the canyon its name. The Santa Fe also had a siding called Gypsum along the tracks across the river, opposite the mouth of the canyon. In more recent years, the area has supported a sand and gravel operation, and has been considered as a site for both a landfill and a jail. In 2005, the City of Anaheim approved an Irvine Company plan for a 3,000 acre residential development here to be known as Mountain Park. The first homes are expected to be available in 2007.

H

Hall Canyon. Over the years, the names of Hall Canyon and Baker Canyon have somehow gotten switched around on maps. W.H. Hall was keeping bees in what is now known as Baker Canyon as early as 1873. Charles Baker came later, and settled in the southern fork of Baker Canyon that is now known as Hall Canyon.

Handy Creek. Owen Handy settled in Villa Park in 1882, and later had a ranch along the street that still bears his name. Handy Creek, which runs through Orange Park acres, was more likely named for one of his descendants — perhaps one of his sons: Joe Handy, a successful farmer and water conservation advocate, or Harry Handy, a one-time zanjero (ditchkeeper) for the Santa Ana Valley Irrigation Company; or perhaps for his grandson, Robert L. Handy, who served on the board of directors of the Serrano Irrigation District for more than 20 years in the 1940s, '50s, and '60s.

Hansen. A station on Pacific Electric line to Santa Ana, near Ball Road and Knott Avenue, now a part of Anaheim. Named for Gus Hansen (1850-1912), a pioneer sugar beet grower. In 1905, when the PE came through, he gave them a right-of-way across his 335-acre ranch west of Anaheim. A small community began to develop here in the 1920s, and the first store opened in 1926. Knott Avenue was originally known as Hansen Road, and Gus Hansen Elementary School and Hansen Park can still be found nearby.

Harbor. A short-lived post office (1914-1915) serving Delhi. John Otto circulated petitions for a post office here early in 1914, and since the name Delhi had already been taken by another California community, he offered a list of 15 or 20 possible names. Harbor was on the bottom of the list, but was the eventual choice. It "was suggested to him by Capt. Kelly, an old salt, who concluded to make Delhi his harbor a long while ago," perhaps with an eye to the benefit the area would receive when Newport Harbor was fully developed (*Register*, April 27, 1914). Otto became the first postmaster. In 1915 the office was moved a short ways north, and reborn as **Gloryetta** (*see*).

Harbor Island. Longtime Newport Beach developer Joseph Beek bought a sandbar known as Williams Island in 1926, raised it by dredging, and subdivided it. In 1943, the five registered voters on the island voted unanimously to annex to the City of Newport Beach. Today it is one of city's many exclusive residential neighborhoods.

Harbor View Hills. An Irvine Company subdivision in the hills above Corona del Mar, overlooking Newport Harbor. Homes here went on the market in 1966.

Harding. A little community south of Lincoln Avenue, between Beach Boulevard and Western Avenue. It was laid out in 1923 by Henry Misenheimer, who named it in honor of President Warren G. Harding, who died later that year. There were a couple of businesses along the highway here, and the place was big enough to have its own correspondent to the *Buena Park News* in the early 1930s. Harding Avenue can still be found here, but almost all the old homes have vanished.

Harding Canyon. Isaac (Ike) Harding (d. 1921) homesteaded in this spur of Modjeska Canyon in 1875. "Harding raised goats and maintained an apiary in the canyon until the homestead was purchased by Madame Modjeska in 1898" (Meadows, 1966:69). During the 1878 Silverado mining boom, a townsite known as Santiago City was established in the canyon. In 1900, Modjeska and her husband, Count Bozenta, had a dam built near the mouth of the canyon, but their reservoir here has long since silted in.

Hargraves Corner. In the 1880s, the street car line from Santa Ana to Orange turned east at Main Street onto La Veta Avenue, a curve that came to be known as Hargraves Corner, after Rufus Hargrave, a local rancher. The Pacific Electric later bought the line, and continued to use the old name until they abandoned service to Orange in 1930.

Harper. The original name of Costa Mesa. "A loading platform and siding on the old Santa Ana and Newport Railroad, established in 1899.... It was named for Gregory Harper, who farmed considerable land in the neighborhood" (Meadows, 1966:69). In the 1890s, Harper and his brother, William, leased the land west of Harbor Boulevard and south of 19th Street to grow grain. But they left the area shortly after 1900. The railroad stop was near Newport Boulevard and 18th Street, and a little community eventually grew up around it, with a formal townsite laid out in 1910. The Harper Post Office operated from 1909 to 1920, when it was renamed Costa Mesa. The Harper School District was formed in 1909, merged with Fairview in 1915, and became the Costa Mesa school district in 1926.

Harperville. A Pacific Electric stop where the tracks crossed Chapman Avenue near Gilbert Street in what is now Garden Grove. A subdivision known as Berryfield was laid out in 1907, just east of the station at Chapman Avenue and Brookhurst Street, but the PE name proved more popular.

Hawthorne. A later name for the Delhi School District, adopted in 1924, and lost in 1926 when the district merged with the Santa Ana city schools.

Hewes Park. In the early 1880s, David Hewes (1822-1915), who had made his fortune as a grading contractor in San Francisco during the Gold Rush, bought more than 800 acres between El Modena and Tustin. Eventually much of the land was planted to citrus. Hewes built a fine home for himself which he called Anapauma, said to mean "A Place of Rest." In 1905, he began development of Hewes Park on a small hill above the northwest corner of Esplanade Street and La Veta Avenue. It was a private park, built for the public as a gift from Hewes. Much of the ranch was subdivided in the 1920s, but Hewes Park survived until around 1940.

Hicks Canyon. Pioneer beekeeper Jim Hickey was the namesake of two local place names. The original Hickey Canyon is near Trabuco Oaks, while Hicks Canyon is in the foothills north of Irvine. "Over the years government map makers have thoroughly screwed up the canyon place names surrounding Trabuco Oaks," Jim Sleeper grouses. "What is now called Hickey Canyon (or Oak Drive),... was originally Weakley Canyon. It was named for Labon Weakly, a pioneer beekeeper, in the mid-[eighteen]seventies. About ten years later, people began calling it Rowell Canyon, for Edward Rowell, by then a resident. What is today Rose Canyon (the road to the Joplin Boys' Ranch) is the *real* Hickey Canyon, named for Jim Hickey, who kept bees here beginning in 1875. Frequently the name was bobbed on old maps to 'Hick's Canyon.' Later it was called Wild Rose Canyon, which (after 1886) was shortened to Rose Canyon, some say a tribute to Rose Havens (later Mrs. William E. Adkinson)" (Sleeper, 1976:165-66).

Hidden Ranch. A wide spot in Black Star Canyon, once home to an Indian village. "The first European to live in the valley was Juan Cañedo of Mission San Juan Capistrano, who, about 1832, built a cabin of sycamore logs. He called his mountain home Rancho Escondido, Hidden Ranch. Over the years the place has been a cattle ranch, a sheep range, a chicken farm, a Shetland Pony paddock, an apiary and a mountain home" (Meadows, 1966:70).

Hobo Canyon. A small canyon north of Aliso Canyon, "Said to have been a favored rendezvous for itinerants who could not ... or would not pay art colony prices" (Meadows, 1966:71). The name dates back to the 1940s, if not before.

Holy Jim Canyon. "Most picturesque of all those [canyons] who were named from pioneers is Holy Jim Canyon, the branch of the

Trabuco that lies against the south side of Santiago peak. James Smith of Santa Ana had an apiary in the canyon. By reason of his unquestioned ability to expostulate in forceful language, he was often distinguished from the other various Smiths by the name of Cussin' Jim Smith, and ironically therefore as Holy Jim Smith" (Stephenson, 1931:47-48). "James T. Smith had numerous nicknames," Jim Sleeper adds, "the most prevalent being 'Lyin'' Smith, 'Greasy Jim,' and 'Cussin' Jim.' It is doubtful that anyone ever called him 'Holy Jim,' at least to his face" (Sleeper, 1976:182).

Horno Creek. "The roof and floor tiles used in building Mission San Juan Capistrano were burnt in kilns located on the western bank of a stream .5 mile north of the mission buildings. The stream, five miles long, parallels Trabuco Creek on the east and enters San Juan Creek south of the mission. The stream was named for the *hornos*, or kilns, that were on its bank. They existed until the 1920s" (Meadows, 1966:71). The modern community of Ladera Ranch now lies at the top of Horno Creek.

Horseshoe Bend. East of Weir Canyon Road, the Santa Ana River makes a big arc to the north. When the Santa Fe Railroad laid their tracks through the canyon in 1887, they had to follow this curve, and the shape gave rise to the name Horseshoe Bend.

Hoyt Hill. The site of one of the earliest rancho adobes in Orange County, traditionally connected with Juan Pablo Grijalva, a retired Spanish soldier who began running cattle along the Santiago Creek around 1800. The adobe was already in ruins by the 1830s. The little hill was later known as Signal Point before William W. Hoyt bought it in 1887 and built his home here. He called his home Buena Vista. It is located above Hewes Street and Rancho Santiago Boulevard in the City of Orange.

Huntington Beach. The long coastal strip from Newport Bay to Bolsa Chica was originally known as Shell Beach. In 1901, when the West Coast Land & Water Company laid out a new town along the coast, they dubbed it Pacific City. In 1903, a group of investors led by Henry Huntington (1850-1927), the founder of the Pacific

Electric Railway, purchased the townsite and renamed it Huntington Beach. A year later, the Pacific Electric's "Big Red Cars" began
regular service here, and the city incorporated in 1909. The area
remained a quiet beach community until oil was discovered in 1920,
touching off a frantic boom. **Huntington Harbour**. A residential
marina developed beginning in 1960 on what had been the site of
the old Lomita Gun Club (founded in 1903). The first homes here
went on the market in 1962.

I

Imperial Highway. First proposed in 1929, the Imperial Highway
was meant to connect the rich farmlands of the Imperial Valley with
the Los Angeles County coast. The route — based in part on the old
Butterfield stage route — stretched from El Centro to El Segundo.
The project had strong support in northern Orange County and other
areas along the way, but only portions of the highway were ever
built. The stretch from Yorba Linda down into the Santa Ana Canyon
(State Route 90) is also known as the Richard M. Nixon Parkway.

Irvine (town). The original town of Irvine grew up around an 1887
Santa Fe Railroad siding at what is now Sand Canyon Road and the
Santa Ana (5) Freeway. The station and the community were known
as Irvine, but because there was already an Irvine Post Office in
Calaveras County, the post office here was named **Myford** (*see*),
for James Irvine's one-year-old son. It opened in 1899, and was eventually renamed Irvine in 1914. In 1965, after the new master-planned
community of Irvine was underway, the old Irvine Post Office was
renamed East Irvine, and the railroad station was renamed Valencia.
Today, the original townsite is known as Old Irvine, and is listed as
State Historical Landmark #1004. Several historic buildings have
been preserved, including the 1949 lima bean warehouse, which has
been transformed into a La Quinta Inn — surely the most unlikely
adaptive reuse project in Orange County. **Irvine** (city). In 1960, The
Irvine Company hired William Pereira & Associates to create a master
plan for the development of the Irvine Ranch. They created a vision

of dozens of residential "villages" spread across the ranch, and construction began. In 1971, the residents of the new Irvine voted to incorporate as the City of Irvine. *See* **Turtle Rock** and **University Park**. **Irvine Cove**. An exclusive gated community above Cameo Cove at the north end of Laguna Beach. A number of the members of the Irvine family have had homes here over the years. **Irvine Park**. In 1897, James Irvine offered to donate a park to the County of Orange. They selected 160 acres under the oak trees along Santiago Creek. The area had been a popular vacation spot with local residents since the 1870s, when it was known as the Picnic Grounds. Being the only one, it naturally came to be known as the Orange County Park. It was officially renamed Irvine Park in 1926, but the new name was slow to catch on (and still hasn't caught on with some old timers even today). Since camping was not allowed in the park, local residents who wanted a longer stay would pitch their tents just upstream in an area they called Camptonville. **Irvine Ranch**. Named for the first James Irvine (1827-1886), who was born in Ireland and came to California during the Gold Rush of 1849. He soon found there was more money to be made selling supplies to the miners than digging for gold, and by the 1860s had amassed a small fortune. In 1864, he joined with Benjamin Flint, his brother Thomas, and their cousin Llewellyn Bixby in buying up land in the Santa Ana Valley for sheep grazing. Eventually, Flint, Bixby & Company acquired the Rancho San Joaquín, the Rancho Lomas de Santiago, and a long strip of the Rancho Santiago de Santa Ana adjoining them. The ranch stretched 22 miles from the Santa Ana Canyon to the sea, covering nearly a fifth of Orange County. In 1876, Irvine bought out his partners, and began to move the ranch into cattle grazing and agriculture. His son, James Irvine Jr. ("JI" to his friends; "Mr. Irvine" to his employees and tenant farmers), inherited the ranch in 1892 on his 25th birthday. He incorporated The Irvine Company two years later, with himself as the sole stockholder. He died in 1947. Until the 1930s, the Irvine Ranch was generally called the San Joaquin Ranch. The family finally sold The Irvine Company in 1977, and gave up the last of their interest in 1983. *See also* **Frances**, **Kathryn**, and **Linda Isle**. **Irvine Terrace**. A residential area along Newport Harbor established by The Irvine Company in 1952.

J

Jamison Spring. A tiny spring below Santiago Peak in the Santa Ana Mountains, named for an early-day hunter.

Joplin Boys Ranch. A correctional facility, operated by the Orange County Probation Department since 1956. It is located on 240 acres of the old Andrew Joplin Ranch. Joplin (1870-1954) was a well-known rancher and miner who settled in the Santa Ana Mountains with his family in 1876. In 1908, he helped to trap the last grizzly bear ever to come out of the Santa Anas.

K

Katella. A school district that existed from 1913 to 1954, located on the south side of Anaheim, near Disneyland. "In 1896 John Rea bought 120 acres of land southwest of Anaheim. To give his ranch a distinctive name he combined the names of his two daughters, Kate and Ella, into a single word, Katella. A road leading to the ranch acquired the same name. In 1913 a Katella School District was formed and a building erected on the southwest corner of Katella Avenue and West Street. The district was absorbed by Anaheim in 1954, but the street name remains" (Meadows, 1966:74-75). Ella Rea (1876-1972) married William Wallop in 1909. Kate Rea (1881-1966) never married. Both were longtime residents of the Anaheim area.

Kathryn. A Santa Fe siding which served the Irvine Valencia Growers packing house, which was located on Jeffrey Road, south of Irvine Boulevard. Kathryn Helena (as in Modjeska) Irvine was the only daughter of James Irvine, Jr. Born in 1894, she married Frank Lillard, but died in 1920. The packing house association was formed in 1926.

Knott's Berry Farm. Walter Knott began growing berries here in 1920 with his cousin, Jim Preston. Later, Knott built a roadside berry stand. In 1932, he planted his first boysenberries — a cross between a loganberry, a raspberry, and a blackberry that was originally developed by Rudolph Boysen. Two years later, his wife Cordelia began serving chicken dinners in a tiny tea room. In 1940, Knott began construction of a western ghost town to entertain the crowds of tourists flocking to Knott's Berry Place (as it was known until 1947). By the 1960s, thrill rides were being added, and Knott's Berry Farm grew to become Orange County's second busiest tourist attraction. The Knott family finally sold the park in 1997. Over the years, a number of other tourist attractions have been built nearby, including Movieland Wax Museum, Kingdom of the Dancing Stallions, Japanese Deer Park, and the California Alligator Farm.

Koreatown. In the late 1970s, a number of Korean-owned businesses began moving to Garden Grove, and eventually a commercial district developed at what was once Garden Square. Today, Koreatown (also called the Korean Business District or Little Seoul) has spread along Garden Grove Boulevard from Brookhurst Street west to Beach Boulevard.

L

La Fábrica. A Mexican-American barrio in the old industrial area in downtown Anaheim, north of La Palma Street and west of the railroad tracks. In Spanish, a *fábrica* is a factory. The Anaheim Sugar Company built a large beet sugar processing plant here in 1910-11, which may be the original source of the name. It was also sometimes known as Sonora Town in the early days.

La Habra. W.J. Hole began selling land in the La Habra Valley in 1894, and by 1895, enough settlers had arrived to justify a post office. The La Habra School District followed in 1896, but it was not until 1903 that Robert Hiatt laid out an actual townsite. The La Habra Post Office closed that same year, but the arrival of the Pacific Electric in 1908 revitalized the town, and the post office re-opened at the beginning of 1912. The City of La Habra incorporated in 1925. **La Habra Valley**. Portolá crossed this valley on July 30, 1769, probably traveling over the hills near Fullerton Road. In Spanish, *la abra* means the pass through the hills. Local historian Esther Cramer says this is the "most likely source" of the name (1969:30), which had gained a silent "h" sometime before the area was granted to Mariano Roldán as the Rancho Cañada de la Habra in 1840. Roldán sold his rancho almost immediately, and eventually it came to be owned by Abel Stearns. In the 19th century, the La Habra Valley was considered to extend all the way from East Whittier to Brea.

La Jolla. A Mexican-American community, near La Jolla and Blue Gum streets in the southernmost tip of the City of Placentia. It was subdivided in 1924. The name seems to be a misspelling of the Spanish word *joya* (jewel), the double "l" being pronounced as a "y."

La Palma. A city, originally known as Dairyland when it incorporated in 1955. The first tract homes were built here in 1965. That same year the community voted to adopt its present name, which was borrowed from La Palma Avenue — a street name that dates back to the 1920s, if not before.

La Paloma. A Mexican-American *colonia*, laid out in 1923 near El Modena. The name means "the dove" in Spanish. The original tract is located on the east side of Hewes Street, between Montgomery Place and Phillips Place — streets named for the subdividers. Like most of old El Modena, it has now been annexed to the City of Orange.

La Paz Canyon. Juan Forster's Rancho Mission Viejo was also sometimes called the Rancho La Paz ("the peace" in Spanish), which gave this canyon its name.

La Vida Mineral Springs. A vacation resort in Carbon Canyon near the San Bernardino County line. "[A] well or spring producing 60,000 gallons of water per day was discovered in 1893 by a Mr. Clark, who, when drilling a well [for oil], struck a fissure at 800 feet that produced an artesian flow of mineral water. The water appeared to have therapeutic value, and a popular resort was developed" (Meadows, 1966:76). A hotel was built here in the 1920s, and the water was bottled for sale as a popular soda, La Vida Lime and Lemon. In the 1930s, the springs were popular with Jewish families from Los

Angeles. The resort was still active in the 1970s, but it eventually closed, and the buildings were demolished.

Ladd Canyon. Harvey C. Ladd kept bees here beginning in 1876. Since Mustang Spring was nearby, he called his place the Mustang Bee Ranch. Orange pioneer Nathan Harwood had previously kept bees here, so the area is sometimes called Harwood Canyon on early maps. It has also been called Mustang Canyon, after the spring.

Ladera Ranch. A 4,000-acre planned community, developed by the Rancho Mission Viejo Company. The first neighborhood, Oak Knoll Village, went on sale in 1999. The community is expected to be largely built out by the end of this year. In Spanish, a *ladera* is a hillside or slope. *See* **Horno Creek**.

Laguna. This widely-used place name began with the small lakes (*lagunas* in Spanish) near the upper end of what is now Laguna Canyon. The name appears in mission records as early as 1827. Natural lakes are rare in Orange County, so the *lagunas* were popular hunting and fishing spots in the early days. Beginning in the 1870s, the name has spread across much of southern Orange County. **Laguna Audubon.** A planned community near El Toro and Aliso Creek roads, developed in the late 1980s. It is perhaps the most contested place name in Orange County. First, the National Audubon Society objected to the name, and the developers were forced to add a disclaimer to all of their advertising (including billboards) explaining that "'Laguna Audubon' has no connection directly or indirectly with, nor is it sponsored by the 'National Audubon Society,' or any of its affiliates." Then, in 1989, the first residents sued for false advertising, claiming they had thought the community was part of Laguna Beach, but they found themselves with an El Toro address. Today, the area is a part of Aliso Viejo. **Laguna Beach.** The first settlers arrived here in the 1870s, and a townsite was surveyed in 1883, but not filed with the county until 1887. The spelling of the name was a little slippery in the early days. The post office was known as Lagona Beach (1891-93), then just Lagona (1894-1904), and finally (since 1904) as Laguna Beach. The city incorporated in 1927. *See* **South Laguna. Laguna Hills.** The hills northeast of

Laguna Beach have been known as the Laguna Hills since at least the 1890s. Developer Ross Cortese adopted the name for his Laguna Hills Leisure World. Before long, other subdivisions began being built around the gated senior community. After a failed attempt to incorporate the entire area in 1989, the neighborhoods outside Leisure World voted to incorporate in 1991 as the City of Laguna Hills, while the senior community went on to become the City of Laguna Woods. **Laguna Niguel**. The name was coined in 1959 when planning began for the development on the southern part of the old Rancho Niguel. Steven Manning of Paine Webber, one of the major stockholders in the new Laguna Niguel Corporation, is credited with helping to select the name. Niguel is an Indian place name, spelled in various ways in the early records. Its exact meaning seems to have been lost. The first residents of the 7,100-acre master planned community arrived in 1962, and the city incorporated in 1989. **Laguna Woods**. In 1962, developer Ross Cortese bought 3,500 acres of the old Moulton Ranch where he developed Laguna Hills Leisure World, a gated community open only to seniors, age 55+. The first residents arrived in 1964. After narrowly turning down incorporation as part of Laguna Hills in 1989, the senior community and some of the commercial areas surrounding it became a separate city in 1999. Since the Leisure World corporation claimed the rights to that name, the new city turned to the reliable old name of Laguna, and voted to name their new city Laguna Woods. In 2005, the residents abandoned the Leisure World name entirely, voting to rename the development Laguna Woods Village. It claims to be the largest gated senior community in the world. According to the 2000 Census, the median age was 78.1 years.

Lake Forest. Originally a late 1960s housing development northwest of the little town of El Toro. The lakes were man-made, and the "forest" was a stand of eucalyptus trees planted by Dwight Whiting in the early 20th century. When the area voted to incorporate in 1991, there was a heated battle over the city's name. Some residents favored the historic name of El Toro, but others argued that it too closely connected with the nearby Marine base. In the end, Lake Forest beat out El Toro by just 170 votes, with a third choice, Rancho Cañada, trailing far behind. But when the victors tried to have the old El Toro Post Office renamed Lake Forest, they found that there was already another post office by that name near Lake Tahoe, so the City of Lake Forest is still served by the El Toro Post Office.

Lansdowne. An early 1920s residential area west of Fullerton near Commonwealth Avenue and Magnolia Street. The first residents selected the name, a contraction of "land is down." In 1927, the community was renamed Fuller Park, perhaps because of its location midway between Fullerton and Buena Park. The population in 1929 was only about 200.

Las Bolsas. One of the five ranchos created out of the Nieto concession of 1784; the name was in use as early as the 1820s. In Spanish, *bolsa* means a "purse" or "pocket," but it is also used in a geographical sense to mean an enclosed or surrounded place — such as high ground surrounded by swamps or water on three sides (Gudde, 1998:42). The Rancho Las Bolsas was granted to Catarina Ruíz, the widow of one of Nieto's children, in 1834. A portion of it later became the Rancho Bolsa Chica, and both ranchos eventually passed to Abel Stearns (1799-1871), an American pioneer of 1829. At one time, he owned all or part of seven Orange County ranchos, but he fell on hard times in the 1860s. In 1868 a group of investors formed the Los Angeles & San Bernardino Land Company (more commonly known as the Stearns Ranchos) to market Stearns' holdings, including the Rancho Las Bolsas. What is now the Huntington Beach Union High School was originally known as the Las Bolsas Union High School (1903-1907).

Las Flores. A 1,000-acre planned community, developed by the Santa Margarita Company. The initial plans were approved in 1990, and construction began in 1991. The name is an import from San Diego County. The original Las Flores was an Indian village, then a mission outpost, an Indian pueblo, and finally a part of the vast Rancho Santa Margarita y Las Flores (today's Camp Pendleton). The Rancho Trabuco, where Las Flores is located, was combined with the Rancho Santa Margarita y Las Flores for many years, giving the developers a connection with the historic old name.

Las Paredes. "Las Paredes, the walls, are mentioned so casually in early records that they seem to be a well-known place, but with the coming of the Americans the name slipped into oblivion.... The Grijalva heirs had an establishment located at the edge of the Santa Ana River. In 1811 heavy rains changed the course of the river and damaged the buildings and corrals, leaving only the adobe walls on the river bank. Signs of civilization were rare in early days and even ruined walls were conspicuous" (Meadows, 1966:77). Meadows locates the site near McFadden Avenue and Ward Street. The name appears in print as late as 1880.

Lasky Camp. Beginning around 1921, Famous Players-Lasky (an ancestor of Paramount Pictures) began filming motion pictures in the upper Santa Ana Canyon, south of the river near the mouth of Coal Canyon. Named for producer Jesse L. Lasky, the spot was used for outdoor scenes in a number of pictures in the 1920s. The area was popular with picnickers on into the 1950s, and the Motor Transit company even had a bus stop nearby in the early days.

Laurel. A school district formed in 1898 to serve the new town of Los Alamitos. There was already an Alamitos School District in Orange County then, which probably accounts for the district not following the name of the town. The district has sometimes been confused with an earlier (1881) Laurel School District, which turns out to have been near Laurel Canyon in Los Angeles County. The local district was finally renamed Los Alamitos in 1953.

Leisure World — *see* **Laguna Woods** and **Seal Beach Leisure World**.

Lemon Heights. "In 1910 C.E. Utt and Sherman Stevens bought about 600 acres of hill land northeast of Tustin and the following year set out orchards and built roads and drives. The eminence was christened 'Lemon Heights'" (Meadows, 1966:77-78). Stevens' Victorian home on Main Street is one of the landmarks of Old Town Tustin.

Liberty Park. A residential community laid out in 1923, southwest of Beach Boulevard and Slater Avenue in Huntington Beach.

Liberty Avenue can still be found here. For many years, the community's best known landmark was Marion Speer's private Western Trails Museum, which opened in 1936. Today, much of his collection is on display at Knott's Berry Farm.

Lido Isle. Before Newport Harbor was dredged, Lido Isle was one of several mud flats that virtually disappeared at high tide. Local developer W.S. Collins sold the property to the Pacific Electric Railway Company, and the flat became known as Electric Island, or sometimes Pacific Electric Island. Oilman and former Newport Beach Mayor W.K. Parkinson then purchased it and raised it by dredging the bay around it. It was then known briefly as Parkinson Island. He subdivided the island shortly before his death in 1927. The next owners gave the island its present name. "The name was adopted from that of an elongated island two miles southeast of the city of Venice, in Italy" (Meadows, 1966:78). The grand opening of the new tract was on July 8, 1928.

Limestone Canyon. Sam Shrewsbury built a lime kiln here in 1862 to take advantage of the natural limestone outcrops. The area has also been known as Rabbit Canyon. *See* **Agua Chinon Canyon**, **Shrewsbury Spring**.

Linda Isle. Once called Shark Island, the island was subdivided by The Irvine Company in 1954 and named after Myford Irvine's teenage daughter, Linda. Residents began arriving in the late 1950s. As with many early Irvine Company developments, the original residents could not buy the land under their homes, but had to lease it from the company.

Little Gaza. A modern nickname for the stretch of Brookhurst Street in Anaheim where a number of Arab-American businesses have congregated, including an Arab language newspaper, *The Arab World*. The area is also sometimes referred to as the Gaza Strip or Arab Town.

Little Hollywood. A 1920s Mexican-American neighborhood in San Juan Capistrano, just north of the Los Rios Street district at the end of Mission Street. The nickname was said to have been prompted by two very pretty local girls who "looked like Hollywood movie stars." The area did not even have paved streets until the 1980s. In the early 1990s, when the city began making improvements here, only 13 families remained in the old neighborhood.

Little Mansions. A Mexican-American neighborhood near Beach Boulevard and Orangewood Avenue in Stanton. It was also sometimes known as Crow Village for the birds that frequented the area when there were still open fields around it.

Little Saigon. After the fall of Saigon at the end of the Vietnam War in 1975, thousands of Vietnamese refugees arrived in Southern California. Before long, some began to settle along Bolsa Avenue in Westminster and Garden Grove. Vietnamese businesses followed, and the shopping and residential area soon became known as Little Saigon (which also served as the title of a 1988 novel by Orange County author T. Jefferson Parker).

Little Texas. Many of the earliest black families to settle in Orange County lived on the west side of Santa Ana, scattered through the neighborhoods on either side of Bristol Street, north of First Street. A small community began to develop in the 1920s with the founding of the Second Baptist Church, but as late as 1940 there were still only 300 blacks in all of Orange County, with about half of them living in Santa Ana. In the years following World War II, more and more black families began moving here. Many of the men were stationed at the military bases around the county, and more than a few of them were from Texas. In Santa Ana, many of these families settled along South Raitt Street, and the neighborhood was nicknamed Little Texas.

Little Tijuana. An early Mexican citrus pickers camp that grew up in the 1910s on the east side of Euclid Avenue on the Bastanchury Ranch, in the hills between Fullerton and La Habra.

Live Oak Canyon. Anyone who has driven this canyon on their way to O'Neill Park is familiar with its lush canopy of oak trees.

The name appears in print as early as 1880. It was originally known as Black Oak Canyon, but live oaks are more prevalent here.

Loara. In 1899, the Southern Pacific changed the name of their original Anaheim depot on the west side of town to Loara, and the neighborhood around it quickly adopted the name. There seems to be no end of theories on just how Loara got its name. Depending on who is telling the story, it might be the name of the wife (or daughter, or sister) of any number of people, or a variation on the Spanish verb *loar*, meaning "to praise, or eulogize," or an acronym for the Loftus Oil and Refining Association, or even Indian word meaning "lost child." Local storekeeper E.J. Mercereau claimed to have convinced the SP to adopt the new name, but never seems to have explained why (Guinn, 1902:984). He was descended from old Pilgrim stock, and so perhaps it is worth noting that Loara was the name of the daughter of Miles Standish, one of the most famous Mayflower pioneers. Loara had its own post office from 1900 to 1907. The Loara School District was organized in 1904, and survived until 1952, long after the SP had changed the name of its station to West Anaheim.

Loftus. "A stop on the old La Habra-Yorba Linda Pacific Electric Railway line at the crossing of Imperial Highway two miles east of Brea. Named for William 'Billie' Loftus, oil operator and part owner of the Graham-Loftus Oil Lease" (Meadows, 1966:79). Loftus was the co-founder of the Graham-Loftus Oil Company in 1898, one of the earliest oil companies in the county. For many years, the voting precinct here was also known as Loftus.

Logan. One of the earliest Mexican-American barrios in Santa Ana, and the site of one of the first segregated schools in Orange County. It takes its name from Logan Street, which was apparently named for Civil War General John Logan of Illinois. After the war, Logan helped push for the start of Decoration Day (today's Memorial Day holiday).

Lomas de Santiago. A Mexican rancho in the foothills east of Orange, granted in 1846 to Teodocio Yorba, who had already been running cattle here in the "Hills of Saint James" for at least a decade. His original grant ran south from the Santiago Creek down to the Rancho San Joaquín, but American surveyors more than doubled its size in the 1850s, carrying it all the way north to the Santa Ana River. William Wolfskill bought the rancho in 1860, and in 1866 sold it to Flint, Bixby & Company. They were later bought out by their silent partner, James Irvine. Because of the question surrounding its northern boundary, squatters tried for decades to claim that the upper end of the Irvine Ranch was public land and open to homesteading. The issue was not completely settled until 1932, when the United States Attorney General validated Irvine's title.

Los Alamitos. The Rancho Los Alamitos was one of the five ranchos carved out of the Nieto concession of 1784. The name means "the little cottonwoods" in Spanish. Governor José Figueroa granted the Los Alamitos to Juan José Nieto in 1834, then Nieto turned right around and sold the rancho to the governor at such a low price that some suggested it was bribe for his favoring Juan José in division of the family lands. In any case, Abel Stearns paid a good deal more when he bought it from the governor's estate in 1842. This was the first of his many ranchos, though it did not become a part of the Stearns Ranchos trust, as Stearns had already lost it to debt a few years before. The old rancho is now divided between Orange and Los Angeles counties. **Los Alamitos**. The modern City of Los Alamitos grew up around a sugar beet factory, built on a portion of the Rancho Los Alamitos in 1896-97. A post office opened in 1897. The school district was known as Laurel until 1953. The city incorporated in 1960. **Los Alamitos Naval Air Station**. The first World War II-era military base located in Orange County, this 955-acre site was selected in February, 1941, and the base opened in April, 1942. Today it serves as a joint forces training base.

Los Bueyes. The earlier name for Weir Canyon. A rough trail through the canyon provided a shortcut over the hills from the Santa Ana Canyon, where Mexican carretas pulled by oxen (*bueyes*) once traveled.

Los Coyotes. A Mexican rancho, part of the Nieto concession of 1784. It was granted to his son, Juan José Nieto, 50 years later. The rancho was later the property of Abel Stearns, and was eventually taken over by the Los Angeles and San Bernardino Land Company (the Stearns Ranchos). The adobe ranch house was located in Buena Park above Malvern Avenue, near the southern end of Lockhaven Drive. It was a well-known landmark along the El Camino Real in the second half of the 19th century.

Los Deshechos. Felipe Carrillo received a grant to the Rancho Los Deshechos from his uncle, Governor Pío Pico, just before the American take-over in 1846. It called for about one league (4,400 acres, *más o menos*) below the Rancho Boca de la Playa in what is now San Clemente. But the grant was never submitted to the land commission established in the 1850s to review all Mexican land titles, and so the rancho was never recognized by the United States Government. Juan Forster later acquired the acreage and added it to his vast holdings. Meadows (1966:80) translates *deshechos* colloquially as "roughlands"; it can also mean melted, or broken into pieces in proper Spanish. *See* **Prima Deshecha Cañada**.

Los Patos. A Pacific Electric stop between Sunset Beach and Huntington Beach, located where Warner Avenue meets Pacific Coast Highway. Until the 1960s, that end of Warner was known as Los Patos Road. Duck hunting was popular on the coastal marshes in the early 20th century, hence the Spanish name Los Patos — "the ducks."

Los Pinos Peak. A minor peak in the Santa Ana Mountains (4,520'). *See* **Potrero los Pinos**.

Lowell. A joint school district, formed in 1906 to serve portions of La Habra and Whittier. The school has always been located in Los Angeles County. In 1894, the Lowell Tract was laid out on the Orange County side of the line. Perhaps like the City of Whittier it was named for a famous author — James Russell Lowell. There is a Russell Street running through the tract.

Lubert. Around 1905, the Murphy Oil Company began drilling in the Coyote Hills. Soon, a "small settlement called Lubert, a name coined from the first names of the first drillers, Lew Bauer and Bert

Schinneller, rose on the Murphy-Coyote property" (Cramer, 1969:183).

Lucas Canyon. "Placer gold was found in Lucas Canyon during mission days and since then the rich field has been worked over at various times by Mexicans and Americans. It was named for a Christianized Indian named Lucas who lived in the canyon.... Good-sized nuggets have been found, but never the abundance reported in folklore" (Meadows, 1966:97). A gold strike in the upper end of the canyon around 1900 focused attention on the area, and early myth maintained that "the Indians obtained gold [here] for the images at the mission in the days of Father Serra" (*Register*, Sept. 1, 1920).

Luehm. A Pacific Electric stop on the La Habra line. It was located where Walnut Street crossed the tracks, next to the John Luehm ranch. Luehm settled here in 1897, "the first of a group of Swiss settlers to make La Habra their home" (Cramer, 1969:95).

M

Magnolia. A school district established in 1895 on the west side of Anaheim. Andrew Baker, one of the founders of the district, settled here in 1893 and named his home the Magnolia Ranch. The original school was located at the northwest corner of Magnolia Street and Orange Avenue. A second, segregated school, was later built for Colonia Independencia. Today, there are nine elementary schools in the district.

Main Beach. The long, curving stretch of sand in downtown Laguna Beach has been known by this obvious name since at least the 1920s.

Mancow Rock. A well-known folk name among the old timers. This brown sandstone ridge, some 60 feet tall, is now lost under the eastern end of the Santiago Dam. As Don Meadows tells the tale: "In the early 1890's a wooden shack nearby was a favorite rendezvous for young men who gathered in the mountains to hunt quail and rabbits. One Sunday when the hunters arrived at the cabin it was discovered that one of their members had brought his girl friend to join the group, much to the vexation of the others. As the swain and his lady were walking near the big sandstone rock a bull charged out of the brush and chased them to the safety of the escarpment. The other hunters were delighted, and later painted a picture of a bull and the words: BEWARE OF THE MANCOW on the rock as a warning that this was no place for ladies. As years went by wind and rain defaced the sign but the name Mancow stayed with the rock till it...disappeared under the dam" (1966:98). On the opposite side of the Santiago Creek stood Castle Rock.

Maple Spring. A small spring north of Modjeska Peak named for the maple trees found here in the early days.

McFaddens Landing. Another name for the original Newport Landing, which was located on the west side of the mouth of upper Newport Bay, near where the Coast Highway bridge now crosses the bay. The landing was operated by the McFadden brothers from 1874 to 1888, when they moved their operations to the Newport Wharf. James McFadden, the first of four brothers to settle here, acquired an interest in the Rancho Santiago de Santa Ana and received 4,000 acres south of Warner Avenue in the 1868 partition. *See* **Port Orange**.

McPherson. In 1872, brothers Stephen and Robert McPherson purchased 80 acres along the Santiago Creek and planted raisin grapes. The venture prospered, and by the mid-1880s they were employing hundreds of men during the harvest season. In 1886, they decided to found a town for their employees, located on the north side of Chapman Avenue at McPherson Road, in what is now the City of Orange. The Boom of the Eighties gave their town a brief boost, but a blight swept through the local vineyards about that same time, destroying the town's chances for success and bankrupting the McPhersons. The community had its own post office from 1886 to 1900, and was a stop on the Southern Pacific's Tustin Branch.

Mesa Verde. A Costa Mesa residential area first developed in 1957. It is located west of Harbor Boulevard between Gisler and Adams avenues. The name is Spanish for "green tableland."

Messenger Hill. A small rise, east of Hewes Avenue and north of Old Foothill Boulevard, in the Tustin Foothills. It was named for Rev. Henry Messenger, the founder of the ill-fated town of Fairhaven in the 1870s.

Metate Hills. The first rise of hills northeast of El Modena, near Cannon Street, contains many volcanic outcrops. As early as the 1860s, the stone here was quarried to make *metates* — the traditional three-legged grinding stones once found in every Mexican kitchen. The area where Orange Park Acres is today was sometimes known as Metate Valley. There was also a Pacific Electric stop known as Metate just east of Garden Grove.

Midway City. A little town located about midway between Santa Ana and Long Beach near Beach Boulevard and Bolsa Avenue. Opening day of sales was December 2, 1923. "Midway City is exactly in the center of nine towns," the early advertisements boast (*Huntington Beach News*, Jan. 11, 1924). "California's Latest Booming Town-Site" was promoted by Long Beach real estate developer John Harper. Many of the first houses here were moved in from Huntington Beach by local oil workers. The little community has had its own post office since 1929. Much of the old tract is still an unincorporated part of Orange County.

Mile Square Park. The military appropriated a square mile of farmland here during World War II as an emergency landing field for the Los Alamitos Naval Air Station. Beginning in 1951, the area was used for helicopter training by pilots from the Tustin LTA base, who called it Mile Square Field. In 1966, the county began acquiring the property for a park. The first section opened in 1970, but the military continued to use the landing field in the center for several years thereafter.

Miraflores. When the Southern Pacific built its Tustin Branch in 1888, the point where it crossed the Santa Fe tracks south of Anaheim was dubbed Miraflores by the railroad. Though there was never a depot here, the name soon spread to the surrounding agricultural area, and was still in use in the 1930s. The junction was located near State College Boulevard and Cerritos Avenue.

Mission Hills. A 1920s tract in the low hills above the high school in San Juan Capistrano.

Mission Viejo (rancho). As early as 1827, the padres at Mission San Juan Capistrano mention the Arroyo de la Misión Vieja (San Juan Creek?), a reference to the mission's former site up the canyon (*see* **Quanis-Savit**). Later, the name became attached to the adobe ruins near the mouth of Gobernadora Canyon. In 1845, the Rancho Mission Viejo was granted to Agustín Olvera, the namesake of Olvera Street in Los Angeles. He immediately sold the 46,000-acre rancho to Juan Forster. The ranch was also sometimes known as the Rancho La Paz. In proper Spanish, the name should be Misión Vieja, but like many of our rancho names, it comes down to us by way of the United States Land Commission of the 1850s, which garbled some of the old Spanish names and created a number of new ones. The rancho eventually became the property of the O'Neill family. **Mission Viejo** (city). In 1963, the O'Neill family and a group of investors formed the Mission Viejo Company to develop a master planned community on the northern end of the old Rancho Mission Viejo. The first families arrived here in 1966, and the City of Mission Viejo was incorporated in 1988. *See* **O'Neill Park**.

Modjeska Canyon. Polish-born Shakespearean actress Helena Modjeska (1840-1909) was an international celebrity in the late 19th century. In 1888, she purchased the old J.E. Pleasants ranch in the upper end of Santiago Canyon and expanded his original cottage into a home and grounds she called The Forest of Arden. Modjeska herself is said to have first suggested the name Modjeska Canyon in 1889, but it did not come into common usage until the 1930s. She lived here until 1906, and today her home is a county historic park. In the 1880s, a Modjeska station was established along the Santa Fe line to San Diego, near what is now Bake Parkway. **Modjeska Peak**. "Soon after the death of Madame Modjeska, a suggestion was made that some canyon or mountain in the Santiago canyon area, where she had her ranch home, called the Forest of Arden, be named in her honor. Forest Ranger J.B. Stephenson accordingly gave the name Modjeska to the northwest peak of the two peaks that make up Old Saddleback, and that name now goes on the maps" (Stephenson,

1931:47). Previously, the peak had been known simply as North Peak.

Monarch Bay. A residential community on the Laguna coast that opened in 1960. It was the first development launched by the Laguna Niguel Corporation. The name was inspired by the fact that the chain of title for the old Rancho Niguel went all the way back to the King of Spain (as do all land titles in this area), so the developers chose a royal theme for some of their names. Crown Valley Parkway is another example.

Moody. A Pacific Electric stop at Crescent Avenue and Moody Street, on the edge of Cypress. Joseph P. Moody settled here in 1896 and farmed for more than 35 years. There is also a Moody Creek nearby that flows into Coyote Creek.

Mormonville. In the 1890s, a number of families from the Reorganized Church of Jesus Christ of Latter-Day Saints settled east of Garden Grove and built a church near what is now the corner of Garden Grove and Harbor boulevards. Soon there were enough families to justify a local school, properly known as the East Garden Grove School and sometimes called the Mormonville School. The church was active here until the late 1910s.

Morro Canyon. "Among Spanish-speaking people, the use of the name 'Moro' or 'Morro,' as a name for a peak or hill is almost as common as the name of sugar-loaf is with Americans. In fact, the two words, 'moro' and 'sugar-loaf,' have much the same meaning, having to do with the shape of the peak or hill. Since Moro canyon opens into the sea only about a quarter of a mile from Abalone Point, the outstanding feature of which is a shapely hill, it seems reasonably safe for us to conclude that the hill was once called Moro or Morro, and that the canyon got its name that way." (Stephenson, 1932:114).

Morrow Trail. Walter Morrow acquired the old Pellegrin mines in the upper Santiago Canyon shortly after 1900. "The Morrow Trail leads easterly from the head of Aliso Canyon to the mines. It was built by Chinese labor about 1889 when Pellegrin owned the mines. It is sometimes called the China Trail" (Meadows, 1966:102).

Moulton Ranch. Beginning in the mid-1890s, Lewis F. Moulton (1855-1938) bought up the pieces of the old Rancho Niguel for a sheep ranch in partnership with Jean Pierre Daguerre. Moulton owned two-thirds of the ranch, while Daguerre had the remaining share. Later the partners expanded their holdings to some 22,000 acres, including much of what is today Laguna Woods, Laguna Hills, Aliso Viejo, and Laguna Niguel. The families sold off their holdings in the 1950s and '60s, and modern development began.

Mountain View. The original name of the school district in the Villa Park area, organized in 1881. The school board minutes credit J.B. Hollingsworth with suggesting the name. It was soon adopted as the name of the community, but when an application for a post office was made, it turned out there was already a Mountain View in Santa Clara County, so the name Villa Park was substituted. The Mountain View School District was renamed Villa Park in 1911.

Mustang Spring. A spring on the western side of Ladd Canyon, known by that name since the 1860s, when wild horses could still be found in the area.

Myford. In 1887, the Santa Fe established a railroad stop on the Irvine Ranch where Old Irvine is today. A little community grew up around it, but when it came time to apply for a post office, it turned out there was already another Irvine Post Office in Calaveras County, named for William Irvine, a brother of James Irvine Sr., so the name of James Irvine Jr.'s one-year-old son, Myford, was substituted. The post office opened in 1899. In 1909, the other Irvine Post Office became Carson Hill, and five years later the Myford Post Office was renamed Irvine. Myford Irvine (1898-1959), known as Mike to his friends, went on to succeed his father as president of The Irvine Company.

N

Nago. A Pacific Electric stop on the Pacific Coast Highway, where Brookhurst Street enters Huntington State Beach. It may be a shortened version of Santiago, a name that appears on some early maps. Nago has no particular significance, but the name appears on the 1949 topographical map of the area, so it continues to show up in books and web sites based on that map. *See* **Celery**.

Nellie Gail Ranch. A 1970s residential development, named for ranch owner Louis Moulton's widow, Nellie Gail Moulton. Her father had once operated a store at El Toro, and she and Moulton were married in 1908. After he died in 1938, she took an active role in the management of the Moulton Ranch. She died in 1972 at the age of 93.

New Westminster. A string of late 1920s subdivisions (at least nine between 1927 and 1929), laid out east of "old" Westminster. Most of the subdivisions were west of Beach Boulevard and south of Westminster Boulevard. New Westminster was one of a number of local communities that grew up in the 1920s along the highways of Orange County as automobile travel became common.

Newhope. A school district established in 1879 west of the Santa Ana River. The schoolhouse was located near the southeast corner of Newhope Street and Edinger Avenue, in what is now the City of Fountain Valley. Don Meadows connects the name with the Gospel Swamp squatters who came seeking a "new hope" in their new home (1966:104). Most of the early references spell the name as two words, but eventually the one-word spelling took over. The school district merged with Garden Grove in 1920, but the community was still known as Newhope as late as the 1950s.

Newland. A Pacific Electric station in Huntington Beach, about a mile north of the beach at Lake Street. It was named for William T. Newland (d. 1933), who settled in this area even before Huntington

Beach was founded. His 1898 home has been preserved as a historical landmark. Newland station was primarily a shipping point for sugar beets. It was still in use in the 1940s.

Newport. In 1870, Capt. S.S. Dunnells brought the first cargo steamer into the old Bolsa de San Joaquín, and the first port was established inside the bay. Mrs. G.B. Perkins, the wife of the manager of the Rancho San Joaquín, is said to have suggested the name for this "new port" between Los Angeles and San Diego (in fact the earliest sources tend to spell it as two words). In 1874, the McFadden brothers took over the landing, and operated it for almost 15 years. It was sometimes called Newport Landing or McFaddens Landing. **Newport Beach**. By the late 1880s, it was clear that McFaddens Landing was not a practical place for a port. Crossing the bar at the mouth of the bay was difficult, and even dangerous at times, and only small ships could enter the shallow bay. So in 1888, the McFaddens built a massive wooden wharf out into the ocean. Most of the residents of McFaddens Landing soon abandoned the old site, and moved to the area around the wharf. Some homes were floated across the bay at high tide. In 1891, the McFaddens completed their own railroad up to Santa Ana, and the Newport Beach Post Office was established. Except for a few fishermen and the McFaddens' employees, the community was largely a vacation spot in the early days. But in 1905, the Pacific Electric reached Newport Beach, and in 1906, local residents voted 42 to 12 in favor of incorporation. In the coming years, local residents twice considered changing their city's name. In 1918, Port Orange was suggested as a new name, and in 1940, a formal vote was held to rename the entire city Balboa. The proposal failed 1,014 to 581. **Newport Coast**. The Irvine Company began planning the development of what was then called the Irvine Coast in the early 1960s. After years of lawsuits, the plans for the upscale residential area were finally approved by the county in 1987, and construction began in 1989. By the time the first residents arrived in 1990, the area had been renamed the Newport Coast. Both Newport Beach and Irvine had hoped to annex the area, but in the end, Newport Beach won out. **Newport Harbor**. Called the Bolsa de San Joaquín in Mexican times, the shallow bay was little more than a collection of marshes and mudflats. Several plans to improve it were developed over the years, and in 1919 the citizens of Orange County approved a major bond act to do the job. But it was not until 1934 that federal money made it possible to fully dredge the bay, and the new Newport Harbor was dedicated in 1936. **Newport Heights**. The first tract in the Costa Mesa area, laid out in 1906. It stretched from 15th to 23rd streets, between Irvine and Newport boulevards. The Newport Mesa Tract was laid out west of it, below 19th Street, a year later. An addition to the Newport Heights tract, south of 15th Street, is still sometimes known by that name. **Newport Island**. One of several small island in the bay, first subdivided in 1906, the year the city incorporated. **Newport Landing**. The original port at Newport was located on the west side of the mouth of upper Newport Bay, near where the Coast Highway bridge now crosses. It opened in 1870, and two townsites were soon laid out on the bluffs above — Newport and Wallula. Neither one ever grew. The McFadden Brothers took over the landing in 1874, and it became generally known as McFaddens Landing. In 1888, they built the wharf at Newport Beach and moved their operations there. *See* **Old Newport**.

Nieto Rancho. In 1784, José Manuel Pérez Nieto, a retired Spanish soldier, was given a concession to establish a cattle ranch between the San Gabriel and Santa Ana rivers, from the mountains to the sea. At more than 300,000 acres, Nieto's original concession was the largest ever made in California. Even after the upper portion was returned to the Mission San Gabriel, he was still left with the grazing rights to over 165,000 acres. Nieto called his ranch La Zanja (meaning "the irrigation ditch" in Spanish), or Santa Gertrudes, but it was commonly known as Los Nietos. After his death in 1804, the rancho passed to Nieto's heirs. Their ownership was formalized in 1834 when the old estate was divided and granted as five separate ranchos — Las Bolsas, Los Alamitos, Los Cerritos, Los Coyotes, and Santa Gertrudes. By 1850, the Rancho Las Bolsas was the only one still owned by the Nieto family. It was purchased by Abel Stearns in 1861.

Niguel (rancho). The only Indian name still in common use in Orange County, Niguel was originally the name of a spring along Aliso Creek, below where it crosses the San Diego (5) Freeway. In mission times, it was used as the general name for this area. Its exact translation is unclear. In 1842, 13,300 acres along the creek were granted to Juan Ávila as the Rancho Niguel. Ávila made a small fortune selling cattle during the Gold Rush, earning himself the Spanish nickname *El Rico* ("the rich one"). But like most of the rancheros, he could not survive the drought of the 1860s, and the Rancho Niguel passed into other hands. Cyrus Rawson managed to buy up all the pieces in the late 1860s, and it was known as the Rawson Ranch. Later it became the Moulton Ranch. **Niguel**. A short-lived school district, formed in 1888. The schoolhouse was located near the junction of El Toro Road and Laguna Canyon Road. A number of families from the Reorganized Church of Jesus Christ of Latter-Day Saints had settled here beginning in the 1870s, and provided almost all the students for the district, which lapsed in 1891.

Nohl Ranch. Cattleman Louis Nohl bought 6,000 acres along the south side of the Santa Ana Canyon in 1943. It was — he liked to say — the largest remaining piece of the old Rancho Santiago de Santa Ana, and so he called it by that name. But most everyone else just called it the Nohl Ranch. Most of the property was sold in 1970 to the developers of Anaheim Hills.

North Tustin. A general name for the residential areas spread across the rolling hills northeast of Tustin. The population in 2005 was about 24,000. Still unincorporated county territory, the area has a Santa Ana zip code, but in 2005 local residents lobbied the postal service to also accept the North Tustin name as their mailing address. The post office also accepts Cowan Heights as a name for this area.

North Yorba. In 1888, the old Yorba School District in the Santa Ana Canyon was divided in two, creating the Peralta and North Yorba school districts on either side of the river. North Yorba was renamed Yorba two years later.

Northam. A Santa Fe Railroad station located just west of Beach Boulevard in what is now Buena Park. It was named for Colonel R.J. Northam, "known locally as 'Diamond Bob,' thanks to his flare for natty suits and radish-sized stickpins" (Sleeper, 1982:86), the sales agent for the Stearns Ranchos when the railroad came through in 1887. His uncle, Edward F. Northam, was one of the leading stockholders in the Stearns Ranchos, owning three times as much stock as Abel Stearns himself. Diamond Bob left Orange County in 1902 and died ten years later. The station was renamed Buena Park in 1929, but the Northam name was still sometimes heard on into the 1960s.

Nutwood. A Southern Pacific Railroad station, located where the Los Alamitos branch crossed Nutwood Street between Cerritos and Katella avenues in Anaheim. It was officially abandoned in 1937.

O

Ocean View (Oceanview). A school district and community, located near Beach Boulevard and Warner Avenue in what is now Huntington Beach. The school district was originally established in 1875, and eventually a little business district grew up here. In 1949, a post office was established as a branch of Huntington Beach, but the community was hit hard by the widening of Beach Boulevard in the early 1950s, which took out nearly all of the local businesses. The post office closed in 1962, but the Ocean View School District has survived to this day.

Old Newport. When the original Newport School District was established in 1871, most of the population was located in the Gospel Swamp area, and the schoolhouse was located near Greenville Street and Sunflower Avenue. A Newport Post Office opened here in 1875, but closed a year later. It was revived in 1882, operating until 1901. After the community of Newport Beach developed, the area was commonly known as Old Newport. In 1918, the school district was renamed Greenville, and the voting precinct followed suit in the 1920s. There was also a Pacific Electric station at Greenville Street and Alton Avenue known as Greenville. The best surviving landmark of Old Newport is the Greenville Country Church at Greenville Street and MacArthur Boulevard, established in 1876 as a Southern Methodist church.

Old Saddleback. "The outstanding peaks of this range as we now find them on our maps are Santiago Peak, the highest, and Modjeska Peak. These two peaks form the topmost saddle of the range, and because of that pioneers of the '60s and '70s gave the two the name Old Saddleback, and that name we use today" (Stephenson, 1931:46-47). "No place in Orange County is held in greater affection by oldtimers than Old Saddleback. From El Toro to Coyote Creek its twin domes are a stable, ever-present heritage on the eastern horizon.... The name Saddleback has been usurped by commerce and industry, but no *paisano* would ever think of shortening the name. It is always OLD Saddleback to those who love the country, and has been so called for more than a hundred years" (Meadows, 1966:107).

Old Santa Ana — *see* **Olive**.

Olinda. The Olinda Tract was laid out in 1887 on several hundred acres north of Yorba Linda and east of Brea. The name is said to be Portuguese for "beautiful," and there is a city of Olinda in Brazil. The Olinda Tract, or the Olinda Ranch, was subdivided into large parcels as farmland. A townsite was laid out near the center known as **Carlton** (*see*), but it did not survive the collapse of the Boom of the Eighties. Then in 1897, oil was discovered on the upper end of the Olinda Tract in Carbon Canyon. The little town of Olinda sprang up, and in 1899 the Santa Fe built a spur line north to serve the local oilfields. Olinda never had a post office, but a school district was established in 1899. It joined the new Brea Olinda Unified School District in 1966. By then, the old townsite had faded away. Many of the last residents were forced out by the construction of the Carbon Canyon Dam in 1959. Today, part of the area is in the Carbon Canyon Regional Park, and a few of the old buildings have been preserved nearby in the Olinda Historic Museum and Park. The modern community of Olinda Village is located about two miles east of the old townsite. *See* **Santa Fe Lease**.

Olive. This area was first settled by the Yorba family around 1810. Since the river and the rancho were already named Santa Ana, the community that grew up here was originally known as Santa Ana, or simply Yorbas. In the 1860s, the area was often called **Burruel**

Point (*see*), after Desiderio Burruel, a son-in-law of Teodocio Yorba. After William Spurgeon founded the modern town of Santa Ana, the community became known as Old Santa Ana. In 1876, the Olive School District was formed, taking its name from either the new olive plantings in the area, or the ancient olive trees growing around the old Yorba adobes. The original school was located on the flats, perhaps as far down as Heim Avenue. In 1882, a flour mill was built up on the hill, powered by water from the Santa Ana Valley Irrigation Company's main canal. In 1887, the owners of the mill laid out the Olive Heights tract on the hill. An Olive Post Office was established in 1887, and except for three months late in 1900, it operated continuously until 1963, when it became a station of the Orange Post Office. Much of the area is now a part of the City of Orange, but a few blocks on the hill are still unincorporated county territory.

O'Neill Park. In 1948, the O'Neill family donated several hundred acres in the Trabuco Canyon area to the County of Orange for a new county park. It was dedicated in 1950. Richard O'Neill Sr. (1825-1910) had come here in 1882 to manage the sprawling Rancho Santa Margarita for San Francisco millionaire James Flood. In return for more than a quarter century of loyal service, he was deeded a half interest in the 200,000+ acre ranch in 1907. In 1941, when Flood's heirs sold the San Diego County portion of the ranch to the government to form Camp Pendleton, the O'Neill family opted to keep its Orange County properties — the ranchos Mission Viejo and Trabuco. Large-scale development of the ranches began in the 1960s and continues to this day. *See* **Aliso Viejo**, **Ladera Ranch**, **Las Flores**, **Mission Viejo**, and **Rancho Santa Margarita**.

Orana. In 1913, local rancher L.E. Smith built a garage at the southwest corner of Chapman Avenue and Main Street, on the route of the new state highway through Orange County. Smith and his mechanic, Otto Buer, coined the name Orana because the spot was midway between Orange and Santa Ana. A "scruffy business district" (as Jim Sleeper once described it) eventually grew up there. The name was well-known on into the 1950s.

Orange. Founded in 1871 by Los Angeles attorneys Alfred Beck Chapman and Andrew Glassell, the town was originally known as Richland. Then it was discovered that there was already a Richland Post Office in California, so the name Orange was selected in 1873. An old wives' tale insists that Orange was named in a poker game, but that story did not surface until 1930 when Margaret Gardner wrote that her father, Henri F. Gardner (who was not here at the time), "told me that he had heard that" a poker game between Chapman and Glassell and two others had settled the matter (Gardner, 1932:160). Others point out that Andrew Glassell's family had once lived on the Richland Plantation in Orange County, Virginia. No doubt that influenced the decision, but historian James Guinn, a resident of Anaheim in the 1870s, is probably closer to the mark when he connects the name to the early efforts to create a separate Orange County. "The agitation for the formation of a new county to be named Orange was quite active about this time. The town of Orange had hopes of becoming the seat of government of the new county" (Guinn, 1902:194). At the time of the name change, there were almost no orange trees in the area, but they spread rapidly after the grape blight of the 1880s, and Orange went on to more than live up to its name. The Richland School District was formed in 1872 and continued under that name until 1879, when it too became Orange. The city incorporated in 1888.

Orange County. The name was first suggested in January 1872, during the second of several attempts to form a new county out of the southern end of Los Angeles County. County Historian Jim Sleeper explains: "to encourage immigration, the area was 'boomed' by real estate promoters as a semi-tropical paradise — a place where anything could grow, and nearly everything was tried. The name *orange* has a Mediterranean flavor about it, so for that reason it was selected to suggest our climate" (Sleeper, 1974:66-67). Writing in 1889, James Guinn was more blunt: "The organizers of Orange County chose that name for the sordid purpose of real estate" (Sleeper, 1974:68). At the time, there were almost no orange trees growing here, and the major cash crop was grapes — both for wine and raisins. The first attempt at county division in 1870 used the name Anaheim County. The 1876 drive suggested the name Santa

Ana County. Orange County was finally formed in 1889. **Orange County Airport**. Opened in 1941, just in time to be taken over by the military during World War II, it was known as the Santa Ana Army Airdrome until it was returned to county control in 1946. Not to be confused with the Eddie Martin Airport, which opened in 1923 a little ways north of here. After MacArthur Boulevard was extended through the Martin site, Martin Aviation obtained the concession to run the new Orange County Airport. Bonanza Airlines began the first regularly scheduled passenger service in 1952. In 1979, at the suggestion of Supervisor Tom Riley, the airport was renamed John Wayne Airport in honor of the late actor and Newport Beach resident. But many longtime countians still cling to the original name. **Orange County Park**. Established in 1897 by a gift of 160 acres to the county from James Irvine. The oak grove here on the Santiago Creek had been known as the Picnic Grounds since the 1870s. The park was renamed Irvine Park in 1926, but the old name persisted for many years.

Orange Crush. Popular nickname (sometimes preceded by an expletive) for the complex junction of the Santa Ana (5), Garden Grove (22) and Orange (57) freeways. More than 65 lanes of traffic meet here, with more than 30 routes in and out of the interchange. The name is said to have been coined by longtime Los Angeles traffic reporter Bill Keene.

Orange Park Acres. A community founded in 1928 by Frank Mead and his partners. The first day of sales was September 15, 1928. The 646 acres were subdivided as acreage, and most early property owners grew citrus and other crops. In more recent years, the area has been known as an equestrian community. Beginning in the 1960s, residents explored either incorporating or annexing to the City of Orange, but in the end, most of the area has opted to remain unincorporated county territory.

Orangethorpe. In the late 1860s, settlers began moving into the area northwest of Anaheim. By 1873, enough families had arrived to justify a school district, which was named Orangethorpe. Like the county and the city of Orange, the name plays on the appeal of the word orange, combined with the Old English word thorpe, meaning a village. For many years, the Orangethorpe School was located at Brookhurst Street and Orangethorpe Avenue. The community briefly incorporated as a city (1921-23), to block a proposed sewer farm in the area, but soon settled back into its rural existence. The city limits ran roughly between Magnolia Street and Harbor Boulevard, south to about La Palma Avenue and north to about a quarter of a mile above Orangethorpe Avenue. The school district was divided between Fullerton and Anaheim in 1954, and the entire area has been annexed to those two cities.

Ortega Highway. It was Father St. John O'Sullivan of Mission San Juan Capistrano who suggested naming the only paved road over the Santa Ana Mountains after José Francisco Ortega, who scouted the trail for the Portolá Expedition of 1769. In an article apparently written for the groundbreaking in May 1929 he explained: "In doing so I wish to point out that it fulfills all the requirements of a suitable name for the road. It is first of all a short, concise name, easily pronounced and remembered and is not duplication, as far as I can learn, of the name of any highway in the state. It is not only a historic name connected with this section of the state, and especially with part of the route over which the highway runs, but it is the name of the outstanding explorer, pathfinder and roadbuilder connected with the very first expedition that came this way" (O'Sullivan, 1929:1). The highway was completed in 1934. According to Riverside County place names historian Jane Davies Gunther, the Santa Ana Mountains are sometimes called the Ortega Mountains by folks on the Riverside County side (1984:365).

Oso Creek (and Canyon). Spanish for "bear," the creek was named when grizzlies could still be found in the Santa Ana Mountains. The name may date back as far as mission times. Several man-made lakes have been built along the canyon, including Lake Mission Viejo and Oso Lake.

P

Pacific City. The original name for Huntington Beach when it was founded in 1901 by Phil Stanton and others. The name was meant to mirror the famous Atlantic City resort on the East Coast. The developers had also considered Bolsa Beach and Superior Beach as names for their new community. Pacific City was renamed Huntington Beach in 1903. The Pacific City School District was established that same year, and adopted the new name three years later.

Panorama Heights. A residential area subdivided in 1927; it was heavily advertised in the late 1920s but remained sparsely populated until the 1950s. Early residents could see all the way to Los Angeles on a clear day. The original subdivision is located between Crawford Canyon Road and Old Foothill Boulevard in an unincorporated portion of Orange County. The name was also applied to the hills to the north above El Modena. The current Thomas Guide street atlas identifies this general area as the Tustin Foothills.

Paularino. Eduardo Polloreno (1824-1912) acquired an interest in the Rancho Santiago de Santa Ana in the 1850s. Polloreno (or Poyorena) was a prominent pioneer in the Los Nietos area and a member of the Los Angeles County Board of Supervisors in the mid-1860s. In the 1868 partition of the Santiago, he received 2,760 acres in what is now the northern end of Costa Mesa. He sold out in 1870. In 1886 about 800 acres of his former property was subdivided for small farms. The tract was located between Fairview Road and the Costa Mesa (55) Freeway, from the San Diego (405) Freeway south to about half a mile below Baker Street. Polloreno's name was phonetically twisted by the new owners, who spelled it Paularino. The population remained small, and there was never a townsite or even a store here. In 1914, a Paularino School District was organized. It merged with Santa Ana in 1957, and the old four-room school building was closed in 1959.

Peatlands, The. A general name for the marshy country in the Westminster/Huntington Beach area, popular in the 1890s and early

1900s. Attempts were made to harvest the peat commercially for fuel here, and there was even a newspaper published at Westminster in those years known as the *Peatlands News*.

Peor Es Nada. The sandy lands along the Santa Ana River south of Placentia were once considered worthless, so they were given a nickname meaning "nothing is worse" in Spanish. Yet Judge J.E. Pleasants recalled people living here when he first visited the area in 1859, and later the Kraemer family had a successful ranch in the area.

Peralta. The Peralta family, cousins of the Yorbas, were co-owners of the Rancho Santiago de Santa Ana. They settled near the northeast corner of the rancho — near Fairmont Boulevard and Santa Ana Canyon Road. The community was sometimes known as Santa Ana Arriba (Upper Santa Ana) but later it was known simply as Peralta. The area was part of the Yorba School District until 1888 when the district was divided, and the portion south of the Santa Ana River became the Peralta School District. It survived until 1940. The 1871 Ramón Peralta Adobe (now owned by the County of Orange) is the best surviving reminder of the community of Peralta. **Peralta Hills**. In 1916, the Jotham Bixby Co. laid out a rural subdivision south of Santa Ana Canyon Road along Peralta Hills Drive in what is now Anaheim Hills.

Peters Canyon. From about 1890 to 1910, James "Dad" Peters farmed in what had been known as Quail Canyon on the Irvine Ranch. In 1896, the Santiago Golf Club was established nearby — the earliest ancestor of the Santa Ana Country Club. In the 1930s, The Irvine Company built two reservoirs in the canyon. Residential development began in the 1980s, but some open space has been preserved in the Peters Canyon Regional Park. *See* **Quail Canyon**, **Santiago Hills**, and **Tustin Ranch**.

Petrolia. A short-lived community in Tonner Canyon, near its junction with Brea Canyon. It was born in 1883, when some of the earliest oil explorations were underway in the area. The name is "a coined word elegantly suggesting oil" (Meadows, 1966:111).

Pillsbury. A Pacific Electric stop in Brea, just west of Berry Street. It was named for George Pillsbury, the PE's chief engineer when the station was established in 1908.

Placentia. This area was originally known as North Anaheim. The Cajon School District was organized here in 1874 but was renamed Placentia in 1878. The name was suggested by Sarah McFadden, the wife of a local school teacher (and no relation to the McFaddens of Newport Beach). It is usually translated as a "pleasant place" and can be found as the name of a few European cities. The Placentia Post Office was originally established in 1893 but was inactive from 1903 to 1911. The actual town of Placentia was not laid out until 1910, after the Santa Fe built a cut-off through the area. The city was incorporated in 1926. In 1962, petitions were circulated to rename the city Valencia, but the proposal never came to a vote.

Plano Trabuco. An alternate name for the Trabuco Mesa, in use as early as 1917.

Pleasants Peak. In 1932, while Judge J.E. Pleasants was still alive (he may even have been in the audience), historian Terry Stephenson proposed to the Orange County Historical Society that what had been known as Sugar Loaf Peak be renamed Pleasants Peak to honor "one of our best known and most respected pioneers, Mr. J.E. Pleasants.... No man has been more closely associated with the history and traditions of the Santa Ana mountains than has Mr. Pleasants. His home has been in the Santiago canyon, in the Santa Ana mountains, since 1861. He is one of the very few '49'ers alive.... We have too many Sugar Loaf Peaks," he explained, "one too many" (Stephenson, 1932:107). The new name was approved by the federal government in 1933. Joseph Edward Pleasants (1839-1934) was one of Orange County's best-known pioneers. At different times, he lived where Irvine Park is today, in Modjeska Canyon (where part of his home is preserved in Madame Modjeska's estate), and then for many years in Williams Canyon. The title of "judge" was honorary — he judged horse races.

Poche Beach. *Poche* is Mexican slang for a dog — the source of the English word "pooch." There was once a railroad siding here between San Clemente and Capistrano Beach on the Santa Fe line known as Poche. Today it is a popular surfing spot.

Port Orange. A 1907 subdivision at the old McFaddens Landing that never got very far. The bluffs above are better known today as the Castaways, after a popular restaurant here that burned down in 1956.

Portola Hills. A residential area developed in the 1980s on the old Glenn Ranch. Gaspar de Portolá was the military commander of the first Spanish settlements in California in 1769. Notice the accent — the name should be pronounced Porto-*lah*, with the accent on the last syllable. The first homes here went on sale in 1986.

Potrero los Pinos. One of three small rancho pastures (*potreros*) in the Santa Ana Mountains granted to Juan Forster in 1845 by his brother-in-law, Governor Pío Pico. The other two, El Cariso [Carrizo] and La Ciénaga, are in Riverside County. Eventually they became part of the O'Neill holdings. Los Pinos Peak, ridge, spring, and saddle all take their name from this spot.

Presita Canyon. The exact spelling of this name would probably tell us more about its origins. The canyon is located on the south side of Limestone Canyon, not far from Irvine Lake. Meadows calls it Presita, meaning "little dam" in Spanish, and says the canyon got its name from a crude earthen dam that once spanned its mouth. Others have suggested the name should be spelled Precito, or damned (in the eternal sense) and trace the name back to two of the Flores bandits who were hanged in the canyon in 1857. Adding to the confusion, the current Thomas Guide spells it Presida, a word which seems to have no meaning in Spanish. Perhaps it is just a phonetic corruption. *See* **Barton Mound** and **Flores Peak**.

Prima Deshecha Cañada. The "first roughlands canyon" in San Clemente takes its name from the vanished Rancho **Los Deshechos** (*see*). There is also a Secunda Deshecha Cañada here.

Puente Hills. In 1769, Portolá's men built a hasty bridge (*puente* in Spanish) to cross San Jose Creek in the Pomona Valley. The name survived as the name of a mission rancho, then as the Rancho La Puente, granted in 1842 to Americans John Rowland and William Workman. Only about 50 acres of this 48,790-acre rancho are now in Orange County, in the hills north of Brea. The name Puente Hills was in use as early as 1857.

Pumpkinville. A nickname for the West Orange area back around 1900. While it was no Gospel Swamp, this area did produce some big crops — including pumpkins.

Q

Quail Canyon. An earlier name for Peters Canyon, coined by hunters who found the little birds abundant here in the late 19th century.

Quanis-Savit. "The Indian name applied to Mission San Juan Capistrano by Junípero Serra, President of the California Missions, when he opened the mission registers in November, 1776. The correct name should have been Sajivit. The meaning is unknown" (Meadows, 1966:113). Because of a lack of water, the mission was moved to its present site in 1778, and Quanis-Savit was crossed out in the registers, and the name Sajirit written in. The original site of the mission (and Quanis-Savit) has been a subject of much speculation, but based on documents uncovered in the 1960s, Meadows (1967) located the original site on south side of San Juan Creek, two miles above the present site, up on a bluff on what was then the Lacouague Ranch. Most of the area was subdivided in the 1980s and built up with homes.

R

Rancho Cielo. A gated community, launched in the late 1980s. Literally, the name means "sky ranch" in Spanish.

Rancho Santa Margarita (ranch). A name originally given to the southern end of Camp Pendleton by the Portolá expedition of 1769, who arrived there on July 20th, the feast day of St. Margaret. The area became part of the Rancho Santa Margarita y Las Flores in the 1840s, which was later acquired by Juan Forster. His holdings also include the Rancho Mission Viejo and the Rancho Trabuco. The entire spread — more than 200,000 acres — was commonly known as the Rancho Santa Margarita. From Forster, the ranch eventually passed to the Flood, Baumgartner, and O'Neill families. In 1941, the Floods and Baumgartners sold their share to the government to form Camp Pendleton, leaving the O'Neills with the northern end in Orange County, which they renamed the Rancho Mission Viejo. **Rancho Santa Margarita** (city). After the successful development of Mission Viejo, the O'Neills formed the Santa Margarita Company, and began planning for a new master planned community on the Trabuco Mesa to be known as Santa Margarita. But shortly before the first families arrived in 1986, complaints were lodged by the town of Santa Margarita in San Luis Obispo County. To avoid confusion, the new community's name was extended to Rancho Santa Margarita. The city incorporated in 2000.

Ranchos. Orange County's Spanish and Mexican ranchos are listed alphabetically. *See* **Boca de la Playa**, **Bolsa Chica**, **Cañada de los Alisos**, **Cañon de Santa Ana**, **La Habra**, **Las Bolsas**, **Lomas de Santiago**, **Los Alamitos**, **Los Coyotes**, **Los Deshechas**, **Mission Viejo**, **Niguel**, **Potrero los Pinos**, **Rincón de la Brea**, **San Joaquín**, **San Juan Cajón de Santa Ana**, **Santa Gertrudes**, **Santiago de Santa Ana**, and **Trabuco**. *See also* **Puente Hills** and **Tonner Canyon**.

Randolph. First a school district (1903-16) and then the original name of the Brea townsite (1903-10). Both were named for Epes

Randolph, Vice President and General Manager of the Pacific Electric Railway Company. The original Randolph School was up near the oil wells in Brea Canyon. The townsite was replatted as Brea in 1911, after Epes Randolph had left the Pacific Electric. The school district was renamed Brea in 1916.

Rattlesnake Spring (and Canyon). Don Meadows, who roamed all over Orange County as a young man in the early 1900s, notes dryly, "The name is deserved" (1966:118). Rattlesnake reservoir at the bottom of the canyon was built by The Irvine Company in 1960.

Red Hill. "Red Hill is an important landmark in Orange County. Located east of Tustin, north of La Colina Drive, this mass of red and ochre colored rocks which stands 347 feet above sea level has had several names. The Indians called it Katuktu, the Spanish called it Cerro Colorado or Cerrito de las Ranas, and the Yankees gave it its present name of Red Hill.... Its redness is caused by cinnabar or mercury ore. In 1884 quicksilver mines were opened on its southwestern point. They were more thoroughly developed in 1927 and were reactivated during World War II" (Meadows, 1966:118). The hill is State Historical Landmark #203.

Republican Bend. In the 1870s, the Gospel Swamp area had attracted more than its fair share of Democrats — many of them displaced Southerners who came to California after the Civil War. More members of the GOP could be found among the squatters living west of the Santa Ana River, an area the Swamp Angels dubbed Republican Bend.

Richfield. An 1888 townsite and railroad station in what is now Atwood. After the Boom of the Eighties collapsed, the townsite languished; but the oil boom of the early 1900s gave it a new lease on life. A Richfield School District was established here in 1915, but soon merged with Placentia. When it came time for a post office, it turned out there was already a Richfield, California, so the local post office was named **Atwood** (*see*), and the community eventually adopted that name.

Richland. The original name for the town of Orange, founded in 1871 by Los Angeles attorneys Alfred Chapman and Andrew Glassell. The Glassell family's former plantation in Virginia was named Richland, and the new town was promoted as a farming community, so the name was appropriate in two ways. It was changed two years later when it was discovered there was already a Richland, California, near Sacramento.

Rincón de la Brea. An 1841 rancho originally granted to Gil Ybarra. Only small portion of it is now in Orange County, in the hills north of Tonner Canyon. Literally, it translates from Spanish as the "corner of the tar," but *rincón* is also used in a geographical sense to mean a small area or nook. *See* **Brea**.

Rios Tract. A tiny (seven-acre) Mexican land grant given to Santiago Ríos (ca. 1800-1877) in 1843 when he was Justice of the Peace in San Juan Capistrano. It was located on the east side of San Juan Creek, north of Stonehill Drive. Not to be confused with the Los Rios Street neighborhood in San Juan Capistrano, the oldest residential area in the county.

Robbers Roost (or Robbers Peak). A rocky outcrop on the ridge near Weir Canyon above Anaheim Hills. It was "a landmark entangled with legends that date back more than one hundred years. The hilltop was said to be a lookout for bandits watching for prey and posses in the country" (Meadows, 1966:120). The site was bulldozed in 1973 during the construction of Anaheim Hills. There was also a Robbers Cave in Fremont Canyon.

Robinson Ranch. Walter Robinson came to Trabuco country in the early 1880s and eventually controlled over 1,200 acres here, which he called the Mountain Meadow Stock Ranch. His son, Louis, continued ranching here well into the 20th century. In the 1970s, the northern part of the ranch was converted into a recreational area known as Escape Country. The first homes in the modern community of Robinson Ranch went on the market in 1985.

Rocky Point. "No longer marked on modern maps, Rocky Point was a conspicuous and well known landmark on the east side of the entrance to Newport Bay before the jetties were constructed at the harbor entrance" (Meadows, 1966:120). Today we know the area as Corona del Mar.

Rodriguez Crossing. The lower branch of the El Camino Real crossed the Santa Ana River here, just north of Chapman Avenue. It was the only safe crossing at high water, and was also used by the stagecoaches of the 1860s and '70s. The name dates from the 1860s, when Francisco Rodríguez settled east of the crossing. Rodríguez had previously been Abel Stearns' foreman on the Rancho Los Alamitos. His adobe home stood until 1919.

Rose Canyon. A short canyon leading to the Joplin Boys' Ranch. It was originally known as Hickey Canyon, after Jim Hickey, an 1875 beekeeper. It also shows up on early maps as Hick's Canyon. "Later it was called Wild Rose Canyon, which (after 1886) was shortened to 'Rose' Canyon, some say a tribute to Rose Havens (later Mrs. William E. Adkinson)" (Sleeper, 1976:166). *See* **Hicks Canyon**.

Rosita. A Mexican-American settlement located along Newhope Street, south of Hazard Avenue in Santa Ana, not far from Colonia Manzanillo. The name was in use by the 1950s. Today, Rosita Park and Rosita School are located nearby.

Rossmoor. A 1,200-acre walled community founded in 1958. The name comes from its founder, developer Ross W. Cortese, better known for his Leisure World developments. With 30 different home models (starting at $18,600), it claimed to be the largest subdivision in Orange County when it opened — and it probably was. The community explored incorporation at least twice, and voted it down in 1960. From 1962 to about 1973, and again from 1978 to 1988, it had its own post office as a branch of Los Alamitos. Currently, it is the most heavily populated unincorporated area in Orange County.

S

Saddleback Valley. A general name for the area from Lake Forest to Mission Viejo in the "shadows of Old Saddleback." The name first appeared in the 1960s, and remains popular today. El Toro historian Joe Osterman said that advertising executive Jerry Price coined the name. An incorporation proposal in 1988 would have combined El Toro, Laguna Hills, Aegean Hills, and Portola Hills into the City of Saddleback Valley, but local voters turned it down.

Salt Creek. A fair English translation of Arroyo Salada, the name of the creek in Mexican times, when it marked the southeastern boundary of the Rancho Niguel. In the 1930s, there was a campground near its mouth known as Salt Creek Camp. Salt Creek Beach was acquired by the County of Orange as a county park, and opened in 1972.

San Antonio. Bernardo Yorba's name for his home and rancho in the Santa Ana Canyon. The statue of St. Anthony from his private chapel is now at the Bowers Museum. *See* **Cañon de Santa Ana**.

San Clemente. Ole Hanson, a former mayor of Seattle, founded this seaside community in 1925. Stephenson says he borrowed the name from San Clemente Island, which had been named by the Spanish explorer Vizcaíno in 1602 — making it one of the oldest surviving place names in California. Hanson advertised his town as "The Spanish Village," and required residents and businesses build in a Mediterranean style, with white plaster walls and red tile roofs. The first day of sales was December 6, 1925. A post office opened in 1926, and the city incorporated in 1928. After a few squabbles with the state, the San Clemente School District was formed in 1931. But by then, the Great Depression had hit San Clemente hard, and Hanson's insistence on Mediterranean architecture was abandoned in 1936.

San Diego Creek. "Called San Diego Creek because the old lower road to San Diego followed its southern bank for a few miles" (Meadows, 1966:121). In 1857 it was referred to as the Sanjón

[Zanjón] del Alisal or "ditch of the sycamores," but that was soon replaced by the current name.

San Gabriel River. The western edge of Orange County barely touches the San Gabriel River as it meets the sea. Originally, the river had been proposed as the boundary line for Orange County, but a last minute change in 1889 shifted the line southeast to Coyote Creek. The river takes its name from Mission San Gabriel, the third California mission, founded in 1771.

San Joaquín. In 1836, José Andrés Sepúlveda petitioned for a Mexican land grant for the area around the Ciénaga de las Ranas, which he received in 1837. Five years later, the rancho was extended down to the Back Bay at Newport. Sepúlveda called his expanded rancho the San Joaquín. In 1864, he sold it to Flint, Bixby & Company (and their partner, James Irvine) for roughly 35¢ an acre. They combined it with the Rancho Lomas de Santiago and part of the Rancho Santiago de Santa Ana, calling the entire 108,000-acre spread the Rancho San Joaquín. The name survived long after James Irvine bought out his partners in 1876. *See* **Irvine Ranch**. **San Joaquin**. A school district, established in 1899 to serve the southeast portion of the Irvine Ranch. The schoolhouse was at Old Irvine. In 1973, the old district was divided between the new Irvine Unified and Tustin Unified school districts. **San Joaquin Hills**. These low hills also take their name from the Rancho San Joaquín. Their highest point, Signal Peak (1,163'), was used as a landmark by early surveyors.

San Juan By-The-Sea. Another one of the Pacific Land Improvement Company's short-lived townsites of 1887, located along the tracks near the mouth of San Juan Creek. It was revived in 1925 as Capistrano Beach. *See* **Serra**.

San Juan Cajón de Santa Ana. A 35,970-acre rancho, granted to Juan Pacífico Ontiveros in 1837. Reportedly, the area had been known since mission times as the Cajón de Santa Ana. In proper Spanish, *cajón* means "box," but in California it was also used geographically to mean a canyon boxed in or hemmed in by hills. The San Juan seems to be Ontiveros' own name for his rancho, just as

Bernardo Yorba named his rancho San Antonio. In any case, the grant was submitted to the land commission as the Rancho San Juan Cajón de Santa Ana, and so it remains. Ontiveros sold part of his land to the founders of Anaheim in 1857.

San Juan Capistrano. Orange County's only mission was originally founded in 1775, but soon abandoned when the Indians to the south rose up in an attempt to destroy Mission San Diego. It was re-established on November 1, 1776, by Father Junípero Serra. It was named for Saint John Capistran (1385-1456), an Italian lawyer and politician who gave up his former life to join the Franciscan order in 1416. Famed as a preacher, he traveled much of Europe spreading the Gospel. He was canonized in 1724. Originally, the mission was located about two miles up San Juan Canyon, but it was moved to its present site in 1778. *See* **Quanis-Savit**. In time, a community grew up around the mission. It was formally organized as a pueblo in 1841. Even in Mexican times, the name was often shortened to San Juan. The original post office here was known simply as Capistrano from 1867 to 1905, when the full name was restored. The city did not incorporate until 1961. **San Juan Creek** flows down from the Santa Ana Mountains to meet the sea here.

San Juan Hot Springs. Once a popular vacation spot, a 1947 study identified ten different natural springs here. In Spanish and Mexican days it was simply known as the Agua Caliente (hot water). By the 1870s it was sometimes called San Juan Capistrano Hot Springs — with the Capistrano soon getting lost along the way. "During the 1880s they were commercialized. Cabins, a swimming pool, and a store were constructed and for many years the resort was a popular place with residents of Orange County. In 1936 the County Health Department declared the resort to be below required standards and ordered changes to be made. The requirements could not be met and all the installations were destroyed" (Meadows, 1966:122-23). A few of the buildings were moved down to San Juan Capistrano. The springs were reopened briefly in the 1980s. Today, much of the area is part of the Caspers Regional Park. Nearby are both Cold Spring Canyon and Hot Spring Canyon. Both names were in use before World War I.

San Mateo Point. The southern tip of Orange County takes its name from a mission rancho, known by that name as early as 1827. In the 1920s and '30s it was usually known as Cottons Point, after millionaire oilman H.H. Cotton, whose Mediterranean-style estate overlooked the point. Cotton's home later became famous as President Richard Nixon's Western White House, and in the 1970s the point was sometimes called Presidents Point.

Santa Ana. Orange County's most widely used place name is also one of its oldest. According to Meadows, the name was first applied to the Santa Ana Mountains by members of the Portolá Expedition, who camped below them on July 26, 1769 (1966:124). It was the Feast Day of Saint Anne (believed to be the grandmother of Jesus Christ) on the Catholic calendar. The name soon spread to the valley, the river, and eventually to several local communities. **Santa Ana**. This was the original name for the Olive area. The Yorba family settled here around 1810, near the top of the vast Rancho Santiago de Santa Ana. After the City of Santa Ana was founded the older community was sometimes known as Santa Ana Viejo (Old Santa Ana) or Burruel Point. **Santa Ana**. A school district, formed around 1855 to serve the little settlements scattered along the upper Santa Ana River and on both sides of the Santa Ana Canyon. Several other school districts were later carved out of it, including Anaheim, Richland, Cajon, and Olive. In 1878, the remaining portion was renamed the Yorba School District. **Santa Ana**. The modern city of Santa Ana began in October 1869, when William H. Spurgeon and Ward Bradford purchased 74 acres of the old Rancho Santiago de Santa Ana. A post office was established in July 1870, but it was not until December that Spurgeon officially platted the townsite. The town grew quickly, especially after the arrival of the Southern Pacific Railroad in 1877. The city incorporated in 1886, and in 1889 was selected as the county seat of the new County of Orange. **Santa Ana Abajo**. Around 1830, the Yorba family began to move out from Old Santa Ana along the Santa Ana River. José Antonio Yorba II moved down the river into what is now the northwestern part of the City of Orange. The little community that grew up here became known as Santa Ana Abajo, or Lower Santa Ana. The settlement had faded away before 1880. **Santa Ana Army Air Base**. A World War

II training base in Costa Mesa, located on 1,300 acres generally between Harbor and Newport boulevards, from Baker Street to Wilson Street. It was in operation from February 1942 to March 1946, housing 2,000-3,000 cadets at a time. There was no flying here, only ground training. Towards the end of the war, the base housed returning servicemen awaiting "redistribution" — reassignment or release. Today, Orange Coast College, Costa Mesa High School, the Orange County Fairgrounds (moved here in 1949), Costa Mesa's City Hall, and many other facilities now occupy the site. **Santa Ana Arriba**. The Peralta family — cousins of the Yorbas and co-owners of the vast Rancho Santiago de Santa Ana — settled in the Santa Ana Canyon in the early 1800s. The community was originally known as Santa Ana Arriba, or Upper Santa Ana, but by the 1880s, it was commonly known as Peralta. The 1871 Ramón Peralta adobe, near Fairmont Boulevard and Santa Ana Canyon Road, is the best surviving reminder of this early settlement. It is now owned by the County of Orange. **Santa Ana Gardens**. A little community near Edinger Avenue and Greenville Street in Santa Ana; it was laid out in 1923. The old Diamond School was located here. **Santa Ana Heights**. A residential area laid out in 1922 by William McCoy. Long a quasi-rural unincorporated area, in 2003 much of the community, along with the neighboring Bay Knolls tract, was annexed to the City of Newport Beach. **Santa Ana Mountains**. While Portolá's men had named them Santa Ana in 1769, in Spanish and Mexican times, Orange County's only mountain range was generally known as the Sierra Trabuco or the Sierra Santiago. The Santiago name survived on into the 1850s, but by then the original name was coming back into use. On the Riverside County side, they were often called the Temescal or Elsinore mountains. The range continues south into Riverside County quite a ways through the Tenaja country and down to Temecula, where they are generally known as the Santa Rosa Mountains, a name borrowed from a Mexican land grant of 1846. **Santa Ana Naval Air Station** — *see* **Tustin LTA Base**. **Santa Ana River**. The longest river in Southern California, it was originally named El Río del Dulcísimo Nombre de Jesús de los Temblores ("the river of the sweetest name of Jesus of the earthquakes") by Father Juan Crespí during the Portolá expedition of 1769. A small earthquake that struck while the expedition was camped near Olive prompted the addition to the Holy Name. But since the mountains from which it seemed to flow had already been named Santa Ana, the shorter name soon won out. The river actually originates high up in the San Bernardino Mountains. **Santa Ana Valley**. Before Orange County was created in 1889, the southern end of Los Angeles County was generally referred to as the Santa Ana Valley. The name survives today as a geographic term for the coastal plain along the lower Santa Ana River.

Santa Anita. A Mexican-American *colonia* west of the Santa Ana River, near First Street and Harbor Boulevard in Santa Ana. The name was in use by 1929, but was sometimes abbreviated Santa Nita. Today the city calls the area Santa Anita Park.

Santa Catalina-on-the-Main. A failed 1887 townsite between Arch Beach and Aliso Canyon in what is now Laguna Beach. "The name was derived from the magnificent view of Santa Catalina Island" (Meadows, 1966:51).

Santa Fe Lease. The main oil lease in the Olinda area, named for the Santa Fe Railroad. The Upper Santa Fe Lease took in the main townsite of Olinda, while the Lower Santa Fe or Olinda Lease was located south of Carbon Canyon Road.

Santa Gertrudes. Part of the old Nieto Rancho, granted as a separate rancho to Josefa Cota de Nieto in 1834. Only about 40 acres of it are now in Orange County. The entire Nieto Rancho was sometimes known as the Santa Gertrudes in the early days.

Santa Ysabel. A Santa Fe Railroad stop near State College Boulevard in Fullerton. Santa Ysabel was the name of C.C. Chapman's famous citrus ranch here, which he named in honor of his first wife, Lizzie, who died in 1894, shortly after they settled in Orange County. Mr. Chapman, in turn, was the namesake of Chapman University on Orange and Chapman avenues in Fullerton.

Santiago. A school district established in 1879 southeast of the Santiago Creek in what is now the City of Orange. It was briefly known as the Amity School District, but within a year was renamed Santiago. The school was located on La Veta Avenue. The district was discontinued in 1895 and its territory divided between the Orange and El Modena school districts. **Santiago City**. An 1870s mining camp in Harding Canyon. It soon faded, and the area was flooded by the construction of the Modjeska Reservoir around 1900. **Santiago Creek** (and Peak). On July 27, 1769, the Portolá Expedition camped on the east side of a creek, about half a mile above where Chapman Avenue now crosses. It was just two days after the Feast of St. James on the Catholic calendar, and so they named the creek Santiago. In early tradition, St. James, an Apostle of Christ, was believed to have first evangelized Spain. As with other early place names, the name soon spread over a wide area, traveling up Santiago Creek to the very top of the Santa Ana Mountains, where Santiago Peak (5,687') is the highest point in Orange County. **Santiago de Santa Ana**. Around 1800, Juan Pablo Grijalva, a retired Spanish soldier who had come to California with Anza in 1775, moved his cattle up to the raw plains along the Santiago Creek. Tradition places his first adobe on Hoyt Hill. But Grijalva died in 1806 without ever receiving a formal concession from the Spanish governor. So in 1809, his son-in-law, José Antonio Yorba, and his grandson, Juan Pablo Peralta, asked to establish their own rancho here. In 1810, they were given permission to occupy the land east of the Santa Ana River, from the Santa Ana Canyon down to Newport Bay. Originally, the ranch was known as the Santiago. Later it came to be known as the Rancho Santa Ana, or simply the Yorba Ranch. But it was presented to the Land Commission in the 1850s as the Rancho Santiago de Santa Ana, the name it has carried ever since. The size of the rancho has caused some confusion. It originally covered some 75,000 acres, but in the floods of 1825, the Santa Ana River moved southeast, and the American courts later ruled that the boundary moved with it. Thus the rancho lost thousands of acres to Rancho Las Bolsas. The Santiago was finally surveyed by the United States Government at 62,516 acres. The partition of the rancho in 1868 set the stage for the founding of Santa Ana, Orange, and Tustin, and opened almost all of the area to settlers. *See* **Lomas de Santiago**. **Santiago Hills**. A residential area developed by The Irvine Company at the top of Peters Canyon in the early 1980s. The area was once part of the Rancho Santiago de Santa Ana. Today it is part of the City of Orange.

Savanna (town). A failed townsite, laid out in 1869 in the Coyote Hills, north of Buena Park, by the Los Angeles and San Bernardino Land Company (the Stearns Ranchos). Much of the community would be in Los Angeles County today if it had ever developed. Historian J.M. Guinn visited the site in 1869 and later recalled, "Long solitary rows of white stakes marked the line of its streets. A solitary coyote on a round top knoll, possible the site of the prospective city hall, gazed despondently down the street upon the debris of a deserted sheep camp. The other inhabitants of the city of Savanna had not arrived, nor have they to this day put in an appearance" (Cramer, 1969:55).

Savanna. A school district established in 1904. The name may have been borrowed from the earlier Savanna townsite, but the school district is actually located well south of there. It serves portions of Anaheim, Buena Park, Cypress, and Stanton.

SAVI Ranch. A commercial area in the Santa Ana Canyon, near Featherly Park. The name (usually pronounced "savvy") is an acronym for the old Santa Ana Valley Irrigation Company, which served the areas around Orange, Santa Ana, and Tustin from 1877 to 1974. The intake for their canal was located near here.

Scully Hill. A point on the Orange County line, north of the Santa Ana River near the top of the canyon. Irish-born Thomas J. Scully was the first schoolteacher in the area in the 1850s, and later married into the Yorba family.

Seal Beach. Originally known as Bay City, the townsite was renamed Seal Beach in 1913, and a new advertising campaign was launched featuring drawings of cute little harbor seals, which lived along the coast here. The city incorporated two years later. An amusement park at the foot of the pier was a popular attraction from the 1910s on into the 1930s. **Seal Beach Leisure World**. The first of Ross Cortese's two seniors-only communities in Orange County, it opened in 1963. There was a Leisure World station of the Seal Beach Post Office here from 1963 to 1970, when the name was changed to Mariner station. **Seal Beach Naval Weapons Station**. An ammunition and submarine net depot, established by the Navy in 1944 on 3,500 acres adjoining Seal Beach.

Serra. A Santa Fe station south of San Juan Capistrano at San Juan-by-the-Sea (now Capistrano Beach), named for the first Father-President of the California missions, Junípero Serra (1713-1784). There was a Serra School District here from 1908 to 1948, when it was renamed Capistrano Beach.

Serrano Creek. A small creek in the Lake Forest area. It was named for the Serrano family, the original owners of the Rancho Cañada de los Alisos. It was called the Cañada del Toro on an 1846 map of the rancho.

Serrano Heights. A residential area in the hills in the northeast part of the City of Orange. Leandro Serrano (d. 1852) married Presentación Yorba, a daughter of the first José Antonio Yorba. When the Yorba family's Rancho Santiago de Santa Ana was partitioned in 1868, his heirs received the portion in the Villa Park area. The name was perpetuated through the Serrano Water Association (1876), the ancestor of the Serrano Irrigation District, which still serves the Villa Park area.

Shady Canyon. Stephenson (1931:51) says that in Mexican times this was called Sombre Canyon or Shady Canyon (properly *sombra*, but Terry's Spanish was not always the best). It was called the Cañada de la Madera (Timber Canyon) on an 1841 map. Don Meadows accepted the "sombre" story with some reservations. The Irvine Company opened an upscale gated community here in 2001 with just 400 custom homesites around a 300-acre golf course.

Sharktooth Hill (also Sharks Tooth Hill). "A name found on no map but well known to youngsters in the early days because of the abundance of fossil shark's teeth that were picked up on its slope," writes Don Meadows, who was one of those youngsters (1966:127).

It was located on the east side of the hills above the El Modena Grade, beyond the present Orange Hills Restaurant.

Sheep Hills. The rolling hills in the northwest part of Rancho Niguel were used for sheep grazing beginning in the 19th century, though this name does not seem to appear until the 20th.

Shell Beach. An earlier name for the Huntington Beach area, it was used fairly loosely in the 19th century to describe the coastline from the mouth of the Santa Ana River all the way up to Anaheim Landing.

Shermanuttville. The San Joaquin Fruit Company's apricot camp on the Irvine Ranch in the 1910s. It was named for two of the major stockholders, Sherman Stevens and C.E. Utt. Apricot camps were common in Orange County in the years before World War I. During a short harvest season each summer, the fruit was harvested, cut in half, pitted, sulfured, and dried for shipment around the world.

Shrewsbury Spring. The only surviving place name to honor the Santa Ana Mountain's second *gringo* settler, Sam Shrewsbury, who arrived here in the early 1860s. His lime kiln gave Limestone Canyon its name. He was the first to keep bees in the canyons, and he had the first homestead at what later became the Modjeska Ranch. He established his home south of Silverado Canyon near this spring around 1877.

Sierra Peak. A minor peak (3,045') at the northern end of the Santa Ana Mountains. In Spanish, a *sierra* is actually a mountain range, not a single peak, so perhaps the name is borrowed from the nearby Rancho La Sierra in Riverside County, another of the Yorba family ranchos. The name was in use by the 1890s.

Sievers Canyon. Actually a part of San Juan Canyon near San Juan Hot Springs, where Henry Siever kept bees from 1887 to 1911. He occupied an old adobe here that some believe dated back to mission times. It was burned out in the big fire of 1993. The canyon has also been known as Decker Canyon after another early settler. A little cabin lease tract occupies the canyon today.

Silver Acres. A community near Euclid Street between Bolsa and Hazard avenues on the western edge of Santa Ana. It was subdivided in 1923. Originally the population was a mix of Mexican-Americans and dust bowl refugees from the Midwest, but it was later known primarily as a barrio community.

Silverado Canyon. Known in Mexican times as Cañon de la Madera (Timber Canyon), the area burst into prominence in 1878 when silver was discovered here. P.A. Clark quickly laid out a Silverado townsite at the junction with Pine Canyon, and served as the community's first postmaster. The original Silverado Post Office operated from 1878 to 1883. It was briefly revived in 1906-07, and then reborn as the Silverado Canyon Post Office in 1931. The Silverado School District followed a similar path. First organized in 1881, it lapsed in 1907, but was re-established in 1916. In 1953 it became a part of the new Orange Unified School District. Mining in the canyons continued off and on for years, but eventually Silverado became better known as a rural vacation and residential area. "During the 1920s several mountain resorts were established in Silverado Canyon, notably Rome's Shady Brook, Lobdell's Mineral Springs, and Hough's Eighty Acres" (Meadows, 1966:129).

Sinks, The. A picturesque jumble of eroded hills and canyons located near the top of Limestone Canyon. It is one of Orange County's most interesting geological features. The name was in use by the 1890s.

Sitton Peak. Named sometime prior to 1900 for J.S. (Sam) Sitton, an early mountain sheep rancher.

Sleepy Hollow. "Old *paisanos* who knew Laguna Beach prior to 1920 will remember the dirt road that became Pacific Coast Highway. Three hundred yards southeast of Hotel Laguna the road dropped into a wide, deep depression, crossed a narrow wooden bridge, and climbed back to level ground. The little valley was called Sleepy Hollow. Dirt fill and store buildings have obliterated this romantic bit of old Laguna Beach" (Meadows, 1966:130). There is still a Sleepy Hollow Lane here. There is also a Sleepy Hollow in Silverado

Canyon, and another is found along Carbon Canyon Road, just over the line into San Bernardino County.

Smeltzer. Daniel E. Smeltzer helped to introduce celery as a commercial crop in Orange County in 1891. Though popular for a time, the celery fields were largely replaced by sugar beets after 1910. A little community grew up around Smeltzer's packing sheds along the Southern Pacific tracks, near Gothard Street and Edinger Avenue (then known as Smeltzer Road). The town had its own post office for just a few months, from May to September, 1900, then rural free delivery began in the area, closing a number of Orange County's smaller post offices. In 1902, shortly after Smeltzer's death, the Golden West Celery and Produce Company bought his holdings here.

Smith Corners. On the old road between La Habra and Whittier, the road made a right turn at Stephen M. Smith's ranch, near the modern intersection of Beach and La Habra boulevards. Smith settled here in 1895, and grew walnuts. His family owned all four corners for many years, hence the plural name.

Soquel Canyon. "A canyon 4.5 miles long with its source in San Bernardino County enters Carbon Canyon from the east one mile east of Olinda. The name is probably a corruption of the Spanish word *sauzal* meaning a thicket of willow trees, which are abundant in the canyon" (Meadows, 1966:130). Oil exploration was carried out here as early as 1900.

South Coast Plaza. In the early 20th century, local promoters took to calling the coastal area from Seal Beach to Newport Bay the South Coast, and the beaches here do in fact face generally south rather than west. When the Segerstrom family began developing a shopping center on their old lima bean ranch in the 1960s, they mirrored the old name by calling it South Coast Plaza. Today the area around South Coast Plaza also features offices and cultural facilities, including the Orange County Performing Arts Center. It is sometimes known as the South Coast Metro area, and some of the local firms even use that name as their mailing address.

South County. A name that has proven rather flexible over the years. Before World War II, the county directories were divided between north and south along a line near Katella Avenue. Forty years ago, many countians would have started the South County somewhere below Red Hill Avenue. Today, others would draw the line at the El Toro Y — and some even further south. While the term South County is common today, one seldom hears places like Los Alamitos or Stanton described as West County anymore. On the other hand, a few people have taken to calling the new housing tracts stretching out the Santa Ana Canyon the East County.

South Laguna. A residential area along the coast, developed in the 1920s. The post office here was originally known as Three Arches (1933-34), but was renamed South Laguna in December 1934. Local residents held a vote to select the new name. On the ballot were Riviera Laguna, Laguna del Sol, and Laguna del Real, but South Laguna won as a write-in candidate by just four votes. The area was annexed to the City of Laguna Beach in 1987.

Spring. The Spring School District was organized in 1869 to serve the central part of the Santa Ana Valley, including the site where W.H. Spurgeon would soon found the town of Santa Ana. The school district adopted that name in 1878, after the old Santa Ana School District in the Santa Ana Canyon was renamed Yorba.

Springdale. A school district established in 1905 above the coast between Huntington Beach and Seal Beach. The name refers to the many artesian wells in the area. The school was located near the northeast corner of Warner Avenue and Springdale Street. The district was annexed to Westminster in 1946.

St. James. A failed townsite laid out in 1887 about half a mile south of Olive in what is now the City of Orange. This was one of several local communities launched by the Pacific Land Improvement Company when the Santa Fe Railroad laid its tracks through the area. The name is translated from the old rancho name of Santiago. It was sometimes jokingly known as "Jim Town." A few buildings were erected, but as the Boom faded, so did St. James. Most of the buildings were moved away, and almost all of the streets were abandoned in 1913. A St. James voting precinct was established here in 1940, and a new subdivision here adopted the name in 1963, dubbing one of its streets Saint James Avenue.

Stanton. When the Pacific Electric came through this area in 1905, a townsite known as **Benedict** (*see*) was laid out near the tracks. The community was a junction point for several branch lines used by the PE and the Southern Pacific. Then in 1911, J.M. Gilbert sold his ranch here to the City of Anaheim, which planned to establish a sewer farm. With the help of Phil Stanton, the community hastily incorporated, and was able to block Anaheim's plans. Stanton later recalled that he "was more than surprised when at one of the meetings of the farmers [by] a unanimous vote, and over my protest they decided to name it after me" (*WPA*, 1936). Philip A. Stanton (1868-1945) was a prominent state politician and land developer at the time. He was one of the original promoters of both Huntington Beach and Seal Beach. Stanton was so small when it first incorporated that it did not even have a post office. The original City of Stanton survived until 1921, and did not re-incorporate until 1956, as residential development began to sweep the area. In the 1970s, and again in the 1990s, proposals were floated to rename the city, but nothing ever came of them.

Starr Ranch. Eugene Starr (1889-1963) purchased 10,150 acres on the eastern edge of the Rancho Mission Viejo between 1927 and 1941 and established a cattle ranch here. Seven years after his death, the land was sold for development. When those plans fell through, 3,780 acres at the northern end were given to the Audubon Society to become the Starr Ranch Sanctuary, and the County of Orange bought 5,550 acres at the southern end to create the Starr-Viejo Regional Park. It was renamed for Supervisor Ronald Caspers soon after it opened in 1974. *See* **Caspers Wilderness Park**.

Stearns Lease. A Union Oil Company oilfield, located on part of the old Stearns Ranchos west of Valencia Avenue, near the mouth of Brea Canyon. In 1909, the company built "houses, store rooms and other buildings" here for its employees, and even planted flowers around the camp (*Los Angeles Times*, Mar. 27, 1909). The lease camp was still a going concern in the 1920s, but by the mid-1930s it was fading.

Stern. The end of the line on the Pacific Electric's La Habra-Yorba Linda branch (1911), located near Imperial Highway and Kellogg Drive. It was named for Jacob Stern (d. 1934), one of the founders of Yorba Linda. The PE had hoped to continue their tracks on through the Santa Ana Canyon to meet up with their line to Riverside, but the extension was never completed.

Stewart. A Pacific Electric stop at Puente street in Brea, named for W.L. Stewart, the Vice President and General Manager of the Union Oil Company, which had a refinery near the station. Their huge oil tanks here burned in a spectacular lightning strike fire in 1926.

Sugar. A Southern Pacific station on the line from Huntington Beach north into the farmlands around Westminster, where sugar beets were once a popular crop. Established in 1907, it closed in 1940. McFadden Avenue was originally known as Sugar Road here.

Sulphur Slide. One mile west of Gypsum Canyon, the Santa Ana River cut into "a high, sulphur-colored cliff under which the road passed. Winter rains caused slides to form and sometimes for weeks the road through the canyon would be closed at Sulphur Slide" (Meadows, 1966:132). The Santa Ana Canyon Road was finally re-routed around the slide after the floods of 1916.

Sun Garden Village (or simply Sun Gardens). A residential tract that opened in 1939 near Garden Grove Boulevard and Newland Street. It was unusual for its time because the developers were building houses rather than just selling lots. The neighborhood was hit hard by the construction of the Garden Grove (22) Freeway in the 1960s, which took out many homes. The area is now a part of the City of Garden Grove.

Sunny Hills. When the Bastanchurys lost their ranch in the hills above Fullerton in the Depression of the 1930s, it was renamed the

Sunny Hills Ranch by the new owners. In 1940 they began subdividing the land into large lots, and an upscale residential area developed here. The area was sometimes jokingly called "Pill Hill" in the old days, because of the many doctors who lived here.

Sunset Beach. A seaside town, founded in 1904 along the route of the Pacific Electric. A post office was established in October of 1905. The community remains unincorporated county territory.

Surfside. A camping spot along the beach here was known by this name as early as 1931. Later a private beach community was developed at the mouth of Anaheim Bay. It was generally known as Surfside Colony in the old days. A post office was established in 1943, and the area was annexed to the City of Seal Beach in the late 1960s.

Sycamore. The original name for the Tustin School District from 1872 to 1890. One of the few native trees here, the area around Tustin was noted for having more sycamore trees than any other spot in the Santa Ana Valley. The supposed "1801" Grijalva map shows an "Alisal" (Spanish for sycamore grove) centered south of Santiago Creek, and the 1868 partition map of the Rancho Santiago de Santa Ana shows a "Belt of Sycamore Timber" ending at the north side of the Stafford and Tustin tract.

Sycamore Grove (or Camp or Flats). A shady spot on the south side of the Santa Ana River, popular with picnickers by the 1930s. By the 1950s, a commercial operation had grown up here, known as the Sycamore Picnic Park. It featured its own miniature railroad. Today, the area is part of Featherly Regional Park (originally Sycamore Flat Regional Park).

Sycamore Flat. The site of Teodocio Yorba's ranch house on the Rancho Lomas de Santiago. The little valley was a popular camping spot in the late 19th century. It was flooded in 1931 by the creation of Irvine Lake.

Sycamore Hills. This area near the upper end of Laguna Canyon has been known by that name since at least the 1960s.

T

Talbert. The Talbert family moved to the Fountain Valley area in 1897, and soon the first few local businesses appeared on their property at the corner of Talbert Avenue and Bushard Street. Tom Talbert, later an Orange County Supervisor, recalled: "Now that we had a trading center and a blacksmith shop at the Fountain Valley crossroads, the need of a post office was badly felt, as Bolsa and Westminster were the nearest places of mail delivery. It was a long drive by horse and buggy and required hours of time just to go for the mail. My father rode a saddle horse while he secured signatures for a petition to the Post Office Department in Washington, D.C., asking permission to establish a new post office, designating the name of the place as Fountain Valley. The petition was returned with the statement that a two-word name for a post office could no longer be used except in case of unusual historical significance. Upon this notification we called a meeting of our neighbors. Some one suggested that we amend the petition and send it back with Talbert as the name for the new post office. We did this. The post office was granted in 1899, and at the age of 21 I was appointed postmaster by President William McKinley" (1952:48). In 1903, the Talberts laid out a townsite at the crossroads. The Talbert Post Office was closed in 1907, but the little community survived. When the City of Fountain Valley incorporated in 1957, the first city offices were in Talbert.

Talega. The original Talega was a post office above San Juan Hot Springs, which lasted just one year — from February 1895 to March 1896. Enough visitors were camping at the hot springs in those days to justify a little rural post office, but the proprietor of the springs was not an American citizen, so Murietta Morris agreed to have the post office in her home (where the Lazy W Methodist camp is now located) and served as its first and only postmaster. Since the Post Office Department frowned on two or more word names, San Juan Hot Springs was refused, and the name Talega was used instead. In Spanish, a *talega* is a "sack" or a "bag," but perhaps in this case it was meant to refer to the narrow canyon, open at just one end.

Talega Canyon. The name appears on maps as early as 1917. There is probably no connection to the earlier post office, except that the same Spanish term is used here. The canyon drains into Cristianitos Canyon from the San Diego County side, and forms part of the county line. **Talega**. The modern planned community of Talega is located northwest of Talega Canyon. Construction began in 1999, and the community is expected to be built out by 2008.

Telegraph Canyon. A telegraph line once ran through this narrow little canyon in the hills north of Yorba Linda. The name appears on maps by the 1890s.

Temple Hills. A residential area above Laguna Beach. Don Meadows says the name dates back to the early 1900s, long before the hilltops were subdivided in 1927. The tract featured its own version of the Hollywood sign, spread across the hill overlooking downtown Laguna.

1000 Steps Beach. A cove below South Laguna, reached by a long flight of stairs. It might seem like a thousand steps climbing back up, but in fact there are only about 200 of them. It became a county beach in the 1980s.

Three Arch Bay. A residential area laid out in 1927 below South Laguna. The arches are in a rock called Whale Island, presumably for its humpbacked shape. The community is now a part of the City of Laguna Beach.

Tin Can Beach. "For many years prior to 1961, when the State of California established the Bolsa Chica State Beach, the long sandy shoreline between Huntington Beach and Sunset Beach was a popular playground for campers and picnickers. No effort was made to keep the beach clean and it became so littered with trash that the popular name Tin Can Beach was applied" (Meadows, 1966:134). Some visitors dubbed it "the poor man's Waikiki."

Tischler Rock. "Near the junction of Niguel [now El Toro] Road and Laguna Canyon Road, a few hundred yards to the east, an adobe house once stood beside a fine spring of water. Sheepmen, running animals on the surrounding hills, made the house their headquarters. On a large rock nearby were carved many names, the conspicuous being H. TISCHLER, July 1860. Hyman Tischler was a Los Angeles dealer in cattle and wool" (Meadows, 1966:134-35).

Tom Thumb Hill. A small round hill at the foot of the El Modena Grade, north of Chapman Avenue. During the Boom days, a street car line stretched from Orange all the way up to the foot of the hill, and the Blount Hotel was built at its base. But the hotel burned to the ground in 1889, and the streetcar line was soon abandoned. In 1980, the City of Orange allowed the entire hill to be bulldozed to make way for a housing tract.

Tomato Springs. Tomatoes grew wild here in mid-19th century, giving the springs their name. They were located just above where the Lambert Reservoir was later built. Tomato Springs first gained prominence in 1912, when a posse tracked an attempted rapist to the springs. Before taking his own life, he shot and killed Deputy Sheriff Robert Squires (the first Orange County lawman to die in the line of duty). Newspapers dubbed the villain the "Tomato Springs Bandit." His identity was concealed at the time, but he was actually Joe Matlock, the son of a prominent family in Eugene, Oregon. In 1932, John B. Joplin established a miniature newspaper he called the *Tomato Springs Gazette*, which he published now and then for his own enjoyment. "Tomato Springs is the smallest place in Orange county boasting of a name," he noted. The name has reappeared recently as the name of two toll plazas on the Foothill Transportation Corridor (241), not far from the old spring. *See* **Agua Chinon Canyon**.

Tonner Canyon. Originally called Cañada de la Brea, it was treated as a separate rancho for many years. But in 1893, the courts ruled it had always been a part of the Rancho San Juan Cajón de Santa Ana. The name Tonner Canyon was in use as early as 1894 — probably from Patrick C. Tonner, a Pomona pioneer who had some connection with the early oil companies in the area. Only a small part of the canyon is actually in Orange County.

Top of the World. A residential area in the hills above Laguna Beach, east of Temple Hills. The name was in use by the mid-1930s.

Trabuco. One of the oldest place names in Orange County. The name dates back to the Portolá Expedition of 1769, when one of the soldiers lost his *trabuco* (a blunderbuss gun) while camped along the creek. The name soon spread to include the flatlands above the creek (called the Trabuco Mesa by later farmers, and the Plano Trabuco by government mapmakers). At times the entire Santa Ana Mountains were known as the Sierra Trabuco. What is now Santiago Peak was still sometimes known as Trabuco Peak as late as the 1870s. Today's Trabuco Peak (4,604') is on the Riverside County side of the mountains. The name was a challenge to early American settlers, who both spelled and pronounced it Trabuca. That spelling was still common long after 1900. **Trabuco** (rancho). The area along lower Trabuco creek became one of the ranchos of Mission San Juan Capistrano. Santiago Argüello (1791-1862) served as civil administrator of the mission after secularization and (as was often the case) was granted the Rancho Trabuco in 1841. He sold it to Juan Forster in 1843, who was granted an additional 14,000 acres in 1846. Eventually, the old rancho became part of the O'Neill holdings. **Trabuco Canyon**. As Trabuco Creek climbs up into the Santa Ana Mountains, it forms a deep canyon. The area was a regular stomping ground for prospectors, hunters, beekeepers, and a scattering of homesteaders in the late 19th century. By 1879, enough families had settled in the area to support a local school, and so the Trabuco School District was formed. Suspended in 1927, the district was re-established in 1942 and became part of the new Saddleback Valley Unified School District in 1973. In 1938 a Trabuco Canyon Post Office was established at Trabuco Oaks. Today it also serves several of the newer neighborhoods surrounding the canyon, including Portola Hills. **Trabuco Highlands**. One of South County's many planned communities. The first homes here were built in 1987. **Trabuco Mesa**. Once an important dry farming area, then a bombing range during World War II, it is now the site of Rancho Santa Margarita. Some maps show it as the Plano Trabuco. **Trabuco Oaks**. A rural subdivision, laid out in 1928. The Trabuco Canyon Post Office opened here in 1938.

Traveler City. A downtown Anaheim barrio. The Travelers were a local R & B band in the 1950s. The name was later adopted by a local car club and eventually became attached to their neighborhood.

Treasure Island. This area was originally known as Goff Island. "Early in the 1870s four Goff Brothers settled on land along the coast south of Laguna Beach. Forty yards off shore...was an island less than one-half acre in extant and 45 feet above sea level. It was thought to be part of the Goff property and acquired their name, but by Congressional action in 1931 it was declared to be public domain and was set aside for its scenic beauty" (Meadows, 1966:66-67). Later the little island was connected to the mainland. Several motion pictures were filmed here in the early days, including portions of "Treasure Island" in 1934, which gave the spot a new name. The old Treasure Island Mobile Home Park here closed in 1997, and the Montage Resort and Spa opened on the site in 2002.

Tri-City (or Tri-Cities). A name used by various community organizations serving Westminster/Barber City/Midway City in the early 1950s. In 1956, it was proposed as the name for a new city, taking in all three towns. Midway City later backed out, but the incorporation election went ahead, and in 1957 Westminster and Barber City voted to incorporate as the City of Tri-City. Five months later, the citizens voted to become the City of **Westminster** (*see*).

Turtle Rock. One of the first "villages" in the master planned community of Irvine, it opened in 1966. It is named for an unusual rock formation that juts out of the ground here. The Irvine Company originally planned to remove the rock, but it survives today in a neighborhood park.

Tustin. Columbus Tustin (1826-1883) and Nelson Stafford purchased 1,360 acres here in 1868, at the time of the partition of the Rancho Santiago de Santa Ana. In 1869, they divided their holdings with Tustin taking 840 acres west of what is now Newport Avenue. He laid out a townsite in December 1870 and named it for himself. The post office was originally known as Tustin City (1872-1894). The

City of Tustin incorporated in 1927, and has grown considerably since then, but much of the hilly land to the northeast is still county territory. Various areas are known as Lemon Heights, East Tustin, North Tustin, Cowan Heights, and Red Hill. **Tustin LTA Base**. Famed for its 171-foot-tall wooden hangars that housed coastal observation blimps during World War II, the base was officially known as the Santa Ana Naval Air Station when it opened in 1942. Most locals simply called it the LTA Base — short for Lighter-Than-Air. Decommissioned in 1949, it reopened as a Marine helicopter base in 1951, and operated until 1999. Today, much of the 2,000-acre parcel is being developed for housing and commercial use. The first new residents arrived in 2004. The City of Tustin has dubbed the old base "Tustin Legacy." **Tustin Meadows**. An Irvine Company development along the east side of Red Hill Avenue, south of Walnut Avenue. It was launched in 1967 — the first Irvine Company tract where the land under the houses was sold rather than leased. At the time, Jim Sleeper was serving as their company historian, and when asked to suggest a name for the new development, he suggested Tustin Meadows — a sly reference to historian Don Meadows, whose book on Orange County place names had just been published. **Tustin Ranch**. A planned community developed by The Irvine Company northeast of Tustin beginning in the 1980s. It includes a number of smaller, gated communities. The northern portions of Tustin Ranch reach up into Peters Canyon.

U

University Park. The first residential "village" of the new community of Irvine, named in honor of the new University of California at Irvine. In 1960, The Irvine Company gave 1,000 acres to the University of California as the nucleus for a new campus. The university purchased an additional 500 acres, and UC Irvine opened for classes in 1965, the same year that University Park went on the market. Today, there are more than a dozen "villages" spread across the old Irvine Ranch, including Turtle Rock, Northwood, Walnut Village, Woodbridge, and Oak Creek.

V

Venta. A 1914 Santa Fe Railroad spur line on the Irvine Ranch, which served the Frances packing house and other points on the ranch. The name is Spanish for "market." The spur was also known as the Irvine Ranch Branch. It was still in use in the 1980s, but it has since been transformed into a bike trail.

Verdugo Canyon. The Verdugo family were among California's earliest Hispanic pioneers. Two of the daughters later married into the Yorba family. Other members of the family settled in this canyon east of the Ortega Highway in the late 19th century.

Villa Park. The little farming community here was originally known as Mountain View, but when enough families had moved in to justify a post office, they found that there was already a community by that same name in Northern California, so a new name had to be selected. The name Villa Park was probably meant to suggest refined country living. The name has always been pronounced like the English *vil-lah*, not the Spanish *vee-yah*. The post office was established in 1888, lapsed briefly in 1900 (when the Post Office Department was trying to close many smaller offices), then continued on until 1906. It was revived as a rural station of Orange in 1964 and (to the delight of local residents) was granted its own zip code in 1996. The area incorporated as a city in 1962 to protect its rural atmosphere, with large lots and almost no commercial development.

Vista del Rio. In 1978-79, the easternmost end of Anaheim Hills explored incorporation under the name of the City of Vista del Rio, borrowing the name of one of the local ranches which dates back to the 1910s. The Local Agency Formation Commission (LAFCO) turned down the plan, and much of the area was annexed to the City of Anaheim a few years later.

Vulture Crags. "Some dramatic masses of yellow sandstone, 2200 feet in elevation, at the head of Live Oak Canyon. Seventy-five years ago [ca. 1890] they were the nesting site of the California condor, now extinct in Orange County" (Meadows, 1966:137). A few of the huge birds were reportedly still seen in Orange County as late as the 1920s.

W

Wagon Wheel. A planned community developed beginning in the 1980s. The name Wagon Wheel Canyon appears on maps as early as the 1940s, and commemorates an old wagon wheel found on this part of the Bryant Ranch. A portion of the canyon was set aside for a county park in 1983 as part of a development deal in Coto de Caza. Originally known as Wagon Wheel Canyon Regional Park, it was renamed General Thomas F. Riley Wilderness Park in 1994, shortly before General Riley retired from the Orange County Board of Supervisors.

Wallula. A failed townsite on the Castaways Bluff above McFaddens Landing in Newport Beach. It was laid out in 1870, but never developed.

Walnut Canyon. The name was in use by the 1940s, suggested by black walnut trees growing here above Anaheim Hills.

Wanda. A station on the Southern Pacific Railroad established in 1888 to serve the Villa Park area. Perhaps it was named for a woman who figured in the life of one of the railroad men — but just who remains a mystery. Local residents objected to the name, and in 1911 the station was renamed Villa Park.

Waterville. An earlier name for the Cypress area, where artesian wells were once common.

Weir Canyon. A weir is a small diversion dam, so the name must come from the water development in the area that began in the 1870s. The canyon's earlier name, *Los Bueyes* ("the oxen"), "probably dates back to the first or second generation of the Yorbas" (Stephenson, 1931:48).

West Anaheim. Beginning in 1875, a community grew up around the new Southern Pacific depot near Broadway and Manchester Avenue. It came to be known as West Anaheim, or simply "the West End." The SP called their station here Anaheim until 1899 when they built a new Anaheim depot downtown. The original Anaheim depot was then briefly renamed Loara before the SP finally adopted the West Anaheim name. The post office and school district here both used the name **Loara** (*see*). Today, the West Anaheim name is used much more generally for the neighborhoods on the west side of old downtown Anaheim, stretching all the way to Stanton.

West Coast Lease. A workers camp for employees of the West Coast Oil Company, located east of Brea near the mouth of Carbon Canyon. The camp included homes, a bunkhouse and boarding house, and a store. It began around 1905, and by 1910 was estimated to have about 150 residents. The residents called the original cluster of small houses "Poverty Row," while the larger homes, built a few years later, were dubbed "Millionaire Row."

West Orange. A little farming community that grew up in the 1870s and '80s in the area west of Orange. The Southern Pacific built a station here in 1880, and the West Orange School opened in 1890 near the corner of La Veta Avenue and Flower Street (a spot now buried under the Orange Crush). Some people jokingly called the area "Pumpkinville" in the old days. Today it is a part of the City of Orange.

Westcliff. A 1950s residential and commercial development along Irvine Boulevard on the west side of the cliffs overlooking the Back Bay in Newport Beach.

Westminster. In 1870, Rev. Lemuel P. Webber (1832-1874), a Presbyterian minister from Anaheim, took charge of some 6,500 acres of the Stearns Ranchos. He founded a temperance colony here, named for the Westminster Confession of the Presbyterian Church. A school district was formed in 1872, and a post office followed two years later. When the area began growing in the 1950s, it was proposed that Westminster, Midway City, and Barber City incorporate together as the City of Tri-City. Midway City soon opted out of the plan, but in March, 1957, Westminster and Barber City voted to incorporate under the Tri-City name. A second election in August of 1957 renamed the new city Westminster.

Whiting Ranch. Dwight Whiting bought up most of the old Rancho Cañada de los Alisos in 1884, and the ranch has been known by his name ever since. The City of Lake Forest covers much of the land today. The Whiting Ranch Wilderness Park opened in 1991.

Williams Canyon. "Once called Cañada Seco or Dry Canyon, it was the home of an early settler named Doroteo Higuirra [Higuera] who was followed by a Marshall Williams, from whom the canyon received its name. Opp Mineral Springs were located in its upper end. For many years the canyon was the home of Judge J.E. Pleasants" (Meadows, 1966:139). The name was in use as early as 1890, and Williams patented his homestead here in 1894.

Willows. One of the names for the area between the old and new beds of the Santa Ana River, south of Garden Grove. The Garden Grove School District operated a Willows School in the area in the 1880s. Perhaps the last official use of the old name was the Willows Drainage District, formed in 1900 in hopes of building canals to carry excess water out to sea from this marshy area. *See* **Gospel Swamp**.

Wintersburg. A small town located along the Southern Pacific Railroad tracks near the corner of Warner Avenue and Gothard Street in what is now Huntington Beach. It was named for Henry Winters (1855-1939), one of the pioneers of the local celery industry. For a brief time, from the 1890s to the early 1900s, celery was one of Orange County's major crops. Winters gave the railroad a right-of-way and depot grounds, and it is said that local residents circulated a petition to have the community named in his honor. The celery fields attracted many Japanese farmers and laborers to this area, and the Wintersburg Japanese Presbyterian Church began here in 1904.

Woodbridge. One of the "villages" developed by The Irvine Company in the late 1970s. By 1980, it was the largest single-family residential project in the city, with 3,500 homes completed, and 3,000 more under construction.

Woods Cove. H.E. Woods had a summer home here in the 1910s. In 1927, his widow gave part of the beachfront to the county, along with access down to the sand through the arch that gives Arch Cove its name. The area above the beach was also known as Woods Point.

X

Xalisco. A flag stop on the Pacific Electric line at Magnolia Street and Indianapolis Avenue in Huntington Beach. Apparently named after the state in western Mexico, where the name is spelled Jalisco. But J and X are sometime used interchangeably in Spanish. Xalisco is an Aztec word meaning "place of sandy ground."

Y

Yaeger Mesa. Jacob Yaeger, a miner, worked for many years in the early 1900s in upper Trabuco Canyon. The mesa named for him is south of his claims and several hundred feet above the canyon floor.

Yorba. A community on the north side of the Santa Ana River, near Imperial Highway and Orangethorpe Avenue, on part of Bernardo Yorba's old Rancho Cañon de Santa Ana. It had a school (located on what are now the grounds of Esperanza High School) and a post office that operated intermittently between 1880 and 1905. During the Boom of the Eighties, a Yorba townsite was laid out along the tracks here, but it never progressed very far. The Yorba School District was annexed to the Placentia-Richfield district in 1930. Today, most of the area is part of the City of Anaheim.

Yorba Linda. A group of investors led by Fullerton businessman Jacob Stern founded Yorba Linda in 1908, and in 1909 turned the marketing over to the Janss Investment Company of Los Angeles. The name combines the family name Yorba (former owners of the land) with the Spanish word for "pretty" — perhaps suggested by the nearby Olinda tract. The Pacific Electric reached here in 1911, and the school district was established a year later. The community became known for its citrus and avocado orchards — and later as the birthplace of President Richard M. Nixon. The city incorporated in 1967.

Z

Zick Place. A 1923 subdivision in Costa Mesa, located along Bernard Street, east of Harbor Boulevard. It was developed by Kathryn Zick, a recent arrival from Colorado. Sales were poor, and she soon left for Los Angeles.

Zuniga Park. Victor Zuniga (1907-1985) grew up in Stanton, and was active in community life for decades, serving as the city's first mayor in 1956. Victor Zuniga Park was named in his honor shortly after his death.

Acknowledgments

No one writes books like this alone — at least, no one should. The past is an awful big country to try and travel by yourself, and I have had many companions along the trail.

Most folks who only read Orange County history will not recognize the name Don Dobmeier, but almost everyone *doing* local history knows the contributions he has made. Orange County place names are a special interest of his, and he has been helpful and supportive through every step of this project.

La Habra native Esther Cramer, who has been working on north county history as long as anyone, also gave the manuscript her careful attention and suggested several new entries. And Jim Sleeper continues to earn his title as our County Historian. His knowledge, his files, and his devotion to our local history are unsurpassed.

Others who reviewed all or part of the manuscript include railroad historian Steve Donaldson, Barbara Milkovich, Doris Walker, my friend Mark Hall-Patton (a place names scholar in his own right), and Chris Jepsen of the Orange County Archives.

Over the years, my research has taken me to almost every library and historical society in the county. I am grateful for all their many courtesies. More recently, I have found myself in charge of one of the premier Orange County historical collections — the Orange County Archives. On lunch hours and 15-minute breaks I have searched the archives for clues about our local place names. I've also had the opportunity to confer with many of the other researchers who come through the door. Special thanks are also due to the Department of Special Collections at UC Irvine, the local history rooms at the Anaheim and Santa Ana public libraries, the Sherman Foundation Library in Corona del Mar, and the State Library in Sacramento.

Selected Bibliography

Armor, Samuel (editor). 1911. *History of Orange County, California*. Los Angeles: Historic Record Co. (Second edition, 1921).

Boscana, Rev. Gerónimo. 1933. *Chinigchinich*. Santa Ana: Fine Arts Press (with annotations by John P. Harrington).

Brigandi, Phil. 1997. *Orange: The City 'Round the Plaza*. Encinitas: Heritage Media Corp.

Carpenter, Virginia. 1977. *Placentia, A Pleasant Place*. Santa Ana: Friis-Pioneer Press (Second edition, 1988).

Chamberlain, H.A. 1971. *The Picture Story of Buena Park*. Buena Park: City Council and Historical Society of Buena Park.

Cramer, Esther. 1969. *La Habra, The Pass Through the Hills*. Fullerton: Sultana Press.

———, et al. (editors). 1988. *A Hundred Years of Yesterdays: A Centennial History of the People of Orange County and their Communities*. Santa Ana: Orange County Centennial, Inc. (Second edition, 2004).

———. 1992. *Brea: The City of Oil, Oranges and Opportunity*. Brea: City of Brea.

Crump, Spencer. 1970. *Henry Huntington and the Pacific Electric*. Los Angeles: Trans-Anglo Books.

Doig, Leroy. 1962. *The Village of Garden Grove, 1870-1905*. Santa Ana: Pioneer Press.

Donaldson, Stephen and Myers, William. 1989-90. *Rails Through the Orange Groves*. Glendale: Trans-Anglo Books (2 volumes).

Durham, David L. 2000. *Place-Names of Greater Los Angeles*. Clovis, California: Word Dancer Press.

Felton, James (editor). 1981. *Newport Beach 75, 1906-1981*. Fullerton: Newport Beach 75th Anniversary Committee.

Friis, Leo. 1965. *Orange County Through Four Centuries*. Santa Ana: Pioneer Press.

Gardner, Margaret. 1932. "The Community of Orange," (in) *Orange County History Series, Volume 2*. Santa Ana: Press of the Santa Ana High School and Junior College.

Gudde, Erwin G. 1998. *California Place Names*. Berkeley: University of California Press (4th edition, revised and enlarged by William Bright).

Guinn, James M. 1902. *Historical and Biographical Record of Southern California*. Chicago: Chapman Publishing Co.

Gunther, Jane Davies. 1984. *Riverside County, California, Place Names: Their Origins and Their Stories*. Riverside: Rubidoux Printing Co.

Liebeck, Judy. 1990. *Irvine: A History of Innovation and Growth*. Houston: Pioneer Publications, Inc.

Meadows, Donald F. 1966. *Historic Place Names in Orange County*. Balboa Island: Paisano Press, Inc.

———. 1967. "The Original Site of Mission San Juan Capistrano," *Southern California Quarterly*. September, 1967.

———. 1996. "Don Meadows *Historic Place Names in Orange County* (1966), Addenda and Errata." Unpublished typescript, author's collection.

Miller, Edrick J. 1970. *A Slice of Orange: The History of Costa Mesa*. Irvine: Hendricks Press (Second edition, 1976).

———. 1981. *The SAAAB Story: A History of the Santa Ana Army Air Base*. Santa Ana: Tri-Level, Inc. (Second edition, 1989).

O'Sullivan, Father St. John. 1929. "Ortega Highway." Unpublished typescript, Orange County Archives.

Robinson, W.W. 1954. *The Spanish and Mexican Ranchos of Orange County*. Los Angeles: Title Insurance and Trust Company.

Salley, H.E. 1991. *History of California Post Offices, 1849-1990.* [Pittsburg, California: Edward L. Patera] (second edition).

Sleeper, Jim. 1971. *Jim Sleeper's 1st Orange County Almanac of Historical Oddities.* Trabuco Canyon: OCUSA Press (Second edition, 1974; Third edition, 1982).

――――. 1976. *A Boys' Book of Bear Stories: A Grizzly Introduction to the Santa Ana Mountains.* Trabuco Canyon: California Classics.

Stephenson, Terry. 1931. *Shadows of Old Saddleback: Tales of the Santa Ana Mountains.* Santa Ana: Press of the Santa Ana High School and Junior College.

――――. 1931. "Names of Places in Orange County," (in) *Orange County History Series, Volume 1.* Santa Ana: Press of the Santa Ana High School and Junior College.

――――. 1932. "Names of Places in Orange County," (in) *Orange County History Series, Volume 2.* Santa Ana: Press of the Santa Ana High School and Junior College.

Talbert, T.B. 1952. *My Sixty Years in California.* Huntington Beach: Huntington Beach News Press.

Talbert, Tom (honorary editor-in-chief). 1963. *The Historical Volume and Reference Works.* Whittier: Historical Publishers (3 volumes; Don Meadows and Mildred Yorba MacArthur, historians).

Tedford, Walter. 1931. "The Tedford Family," (in) *Orange County History Series, Volume 1.* Santa Ana: Press of the Santa Ana High School and Junior College.

Turnbull, Karen Wilson. 1977. *Three Arch Bay: An Illustrated History.* Santa Ana: Friis-Pioneer Press.

――――. 1987. *The Cottages and Castles of Laguna.* Laguna Beach: Copy Cats.

Walker, Doris. 1981. *Dana Point Harbor/Capistrano Bay: Home Port for Romance.* Dana Point: To-The-Point Press (Third edition, 1987).

[Wilson, John Albert]. 1880. *History of Los Angeles County, California*. Oakland: Thompson & West.

Works Progress Administration. 1936. *Orange County Historical Research Project*. Volume 4: Cities and Towns. Santa Ana: United States Works Progress Administration.

Ziebell, Bob. 1994. *Fullerton: A Pictorial History*. Virginia Beach: The Donning Company Publishers.

Newspapers

Anaheim Gazette

Huntington Beach News

Los Angeles Times

Orange Daily News

Santa Ana Register

SUNBELT PUBLICATIONS

"Adventures in the Natural History and Cultural Heritage
of the Californias"
Series Editor—Lowell Lindsay

Southern California Series:

Orange County Place Names A to Z	Brigandi
Fire, Chaparral, and Survival in Southern California	Halsey
California's El Camino Real and Its Historic Bells	Kurillo
Mission Memoirs: Reflections on California's Past	Ruscin
Campgrounds of Santa Barbara and Ventura Counties	Tyler
Campgrounds of Los Angeles and Orange Counties	Tyler
The Sugar Bear Story: A Chumash Tale	Yee/Ygnacio-De Soto

California Desert Series:

Fossil Treasures of the Anza-Borrego Desert	Jefferson, Lindsay, eds.
Anza-Borrego A To Z: People, Places, and Things	D.Lindsay
Marshal South and the Ghost Mountain Chronicles	D. Lindsay
*The Anza-Borrego Desert Region (*Wilderness Press*)*	L. and D. Lindsay
Palm Springs Oasis: A Photographic Essay	Lawson
Palm Springs Legends	Niemann
Desert Lore of Southern California	Pepper
Peaks, Palms, and Picnics: Journeys in Coachella Valley	Pyle

Baja California/Mexico Series:

Cave Paintings of Baja California	Crosby
Gateway to Alta California	Crosby
The Kelemen Journals	Kelemen
Journey with a Baja Burro	Mackintosh
*Houses of Los Cabos (*Amaroma*)*	Martinez, ed.
*Houses by the Sea (*Amaroma*)*	Martinez, ed.
Baja Legends: Historic Characters, Events, Locations	Niemann
*Loreto, Baja California: First Capital (*Tio Press*)*	O'Neil
Spanish Lingo for the Savvy Gringo	Reid
Tequila, Lemon, and Salt	Reveles
Mexican Slang Plus Graffiti	Robinson

San Diego Series:

Rise and Fall of San Diego: 150 Million Years	Abbott
More Adventures with Kids in San Diego	Botello, Paxton
Weekend Driver San Diego	Brandais
Mission Trails Regional Park Trail Map	Cook
Cycling San Diego	Copp, Schad
San Diego: California's Cornerstone	Engstrand
A Good Camp: Gold Mines of Julian and the Cuyamacas	Fetzer
San Diego County Place Names A to Z	Fetzer
San Diego Mountain Bike Guide	Greenstadt
Louis Rose: San Diego's First Jewish Settler	Harrison
San Diego Legends	Innis
My Ancestors' Village	Labastida
Leave Only Paw Prints: Dog Hikes in San Diego County	Lawrence
San Diego: An Introduction to the Region	Pryde
Pacific Peaks and Picnics	Pyle
San Diego Architecture Guide (SDAF)	Sutro
Campgrounds of San Diego County	Tyler

Sunbelt Publications

Incorporated in 1988 with roots in publishing since 1973, Sunbelt produces and distributes natural science and outdoor guidebooks, regional histories and reference books, plus pictorials and stories that celebrate the land and its people.

Our publishing program focuses on the Californias which are today three states in two nations sharing one Pacific shore. Sunbelt books help to discover and conserve the natural and historical heritage of unique regions on the frontiers of adventure and learning. Our books guide readers into distinctive communities and special places, both natural and man-made.

We carry hundreds of books on San Diego and southern California!

Visit us online at:

www.sunbeltbooks.com